THE ORAL HISTORY OF Adm. Jay L. Johnson, USN (Ret.)

INTERVIEWED BY
Jim Robbins

U.S. Naval Institute • Annapolis, Maryland

Copyright © 2018

Preface

People ask Admiral (ret.) Jay Johnson, "when you graduated from the Naval Academy, did you want to be an admiral?" He says, "no, I wanted to be a fighter pilot. And guess what? I was."

Talking to Adm. Johnson, you get the sense that he is a natural aviator. He was born in 1946, the first year of the "baby boom," and grew up in Wisconsin in the 1950s. As a kid, he had been intrigued by his family connections to the military—his father had been an Army Air Force aircraft mechanic during World War Two, and he had a cousin who went to West Point. But what sealed the deal was seeing the U.S. Air Force Thunderbirds perform at a Boy Scout Jamboree in Colorado in 1960. From that point on, Adm. Johnson knew he wanted to be a pilot. He tried and failed to secure a slot at the U.S. Air Force Academy, but their loss was the Navy's gain, as he shipped off to Annapolis as a member of the storied Class of 1968.

Life at the Naval Academy gave Jay Johnson what he admits was some necessary discipline and focus. It also thrust him into the challenging world of carrier aviation, where he excelled as both a pilot and an officer. Like many of his classmates, he soon deployed to the Southeast Asian theater. His combat tours of duty during the Vietnam War, principally aboard the *USS Oriskany*, gave Adm. Johnson battle experience and exposed him to inspiring leaders such as Rear Admiral John Curtis Barrow. He also early on learned the costs of war, as some of his shipmates and classmates either wound up in enemy prisoner of war camps, or never came home.

The mid-70s were a difficult time to pursue a military career. Adm. Johnson experienced firsthand the hostility of certain segments of the public, for example having "all manner of really bad stuff" dumped on his ship while passing under the Golden Gate bridge. After his first decade in the service morale was low, defense budgets were being cut, and many people were getting out. But as he said, "I wanted to fly pointy-nosed airplanes off carriers," and a civilian job as an airline pilot wasn't going to cut it.

Adm. Johnson rose through the ranks into the 1980s, assuming new duties and serving in various command billets. He experienced Cold War missions like shadowing Soviet Bear bombers. And he was an air wing commander during Operation El Dorado Canyon in April 1986, the punitive strikes on Benghazi and Tripoli, Libya, after the La Belle discothèque terrorist bombing in Berlin. The transcript of the interview does not fully convey the animated way in which Adm. Johnson described that mission, using his hands to indicate the relative positions of the different aircraft, in the way that all aviators do.

Adm. Johnson was at the forefront of the transformations of his day. He was one of the first "Super CAGs," when then-Navy Secretary John Lehman made "Air Wing Command a major command at the O-6 level instead of a bonus command at the O-5 level." He later helped testing the then-new operational concept of the USMC Special MAGTF, embarking Marines on carriers with the air wing. As he noted, one byproduct of having Marines on board was inspiring sailors to improve their own fitness regimen.

Adm. Johnson was indirectly affected by the 1991 Tailhook scandal; he had given a briefing earlier in his role as a Rear Admiral (lower half) and head of Navy distribution, but had departed before "all hell broke loose." Nevertheless, this issue came up five years later at his

Senate confirmation hearing for Chief of Naval Operations. As he noted, "naval aviation paid a horrible price for it."

Adm. Johnson was the Deputy Commander of the joint task force assembled for Operation Uphold Democracy, the U.S.-led intervention in Haiti, from September 1994 to March 1995. This was a highly successful test case in exploiting new Joint capabilities and doctrine, and while Adm. Johnson supports Jointness as an operational concept, he also notes how creeping bureaucracy and proliferating Joint requirements have stifled career development within the services. He is very much a Navy man, and discusses the importance of maintaining separate service cultures and traditions for mission effectiveness, as well as morale.

Adm. Johnson spoke emotionally of the tragic suicide of his predecessor as CNO Adm. Jeremy M. Boorda in May 1996. Adm. Boorda was the first prior-enlisted officer to rise to the top rank in the Navy, and Adm. Johnson said his inspirational effect on the sailors was "magical." Adm. Johnson as Vice Chief assumed the temporary CNO post, and so impressed President Bill Clinton that he was made full Chief on June 5, 1996, his 50th birthday. It was the need for the Navy to move past this tragedy that helped inspire his concept "Steer by the Stars," to look up and to the future and not be guided by the wake.

As CNO, Adm. Johnson used his background as an aviator to fight for the F/A-18E and F/A-18F Super Hornet as a replacement for the much-loved F-14, and bridge to the still-troubled Joint Strike Fighter. He also stressed the importance of maintaining a dominant blue-water fleet. He reiterates in the interview that "ship numbers matter" and "to an ally who's counting on the United States Navy to be there, knowing that there's a carrier battle group—you pick the range—50 miles, 100 miles from my shore, ready to help me, makes all the difference in the world."

After his retirement in 2000, Adm. Johnson stepped into important senior executive roles in the energy sector and later as CEO of General Dynamics. He remains active in the military community at large, and also as a supporter of Scouting, being a proud recipient of the Distinguished Eagle Scout Award. He values his memories of his time in the service, and even as he says he is "steering by new stars," Adm. Johnson noted he has "that treasure chest of Navy that nobody can ever take away from me, and anytime I want to open it up and relive part of it or think about it or whatever, celebrate it, bitch about it, whatever it might be, it's mine to do."

James S. Robbins
July, 2017

The U.S. Naval Institute Oral History Program

Researchers and authors have been drawing on the Naval Institute's Oral History Program since 1969, the year it was established by Dr. John T. Mason Jr. He and his successor, author and historian Paul Stillwell, sought to capture, preserve, and disseminate a permanent record of the stories of significant figures in U.S. naval history. Under the leadership of Vice Adm. Peter H. Daly, U.S. Navy (Ret.), CEO of the Institute, the program has expanded, with increasing numbers of historians conducting more interviews.

These oral histories are carefully fact-checked and reviewed by both historians and interview subjects before they are made available. The Naval Institute is known for this high level of editorial intervention and polishing. The reader is reminded, as with all oral history interviews, that this is a record of the spoken word.

The Naval Institute wishes to acknowledge the many donors who make this program possible, in particular the generous support of the Pritzker Military Foundation of Chicago and Jack C. Taylor of St. Louis.

Interviewee Bio

**Admiral Jay Lynn Johnson
United States Navy (Retired)**

Admiral Jay Lynn Johnson was the 26th Chief of Naval Operations, serving August 1996 to July 2000.

Admiral Johnson was born in Great Falls, Montana, June 5, 1946, and raised in West Salem, Wisconsin. Admiral Johnson is a 1968 graduate of the United States Naval Academy. Upon completion of flight training, he was designated a Naval Aviator in 1969.

Admiral Johnson's first sea duty tour was aboard USS Oriskany, where he made two combat cruises flying the F8J Crusader with VF-191. He flew 150 combat missions during the Vietnam War. Subsequent squadron and sea duty tours after transitioning to the F-14 Tomcat included: VF-142, VF-101, Commanding Officer of VF-84; Commander, Carrier Air Wing ONE; Assistant Chief of Staff for Operations for Commander, SIXTH Fleet; and Commander, Carrier Air Wing ONE as Senior Air Wing Commander. His shore duty assignments included: Aviation Junior Officer Detailer; Armed Forces Staff College; Head, Aviation Junior Officer Assignment Branch; and the Chief of Naval Operations Strategic Studies Group.

Admiral Johnson's first Flag Officer assignment was as Assistant Chief of Naval Personnel for Distribution in the Bureau of Naval Personnel. In October 1992, he reported as Commander, Carrier Group EIGHT/Commander, USS Theodore Roosevelt Battle Group. In July 1994, he was assigned as Commander, SECOND Fleet/Commander, Striking Fleet Atlantic/Commander, Joint Task Force 120.

In March 1996, Admiral Johnson reported for duty as the 28th Vice Chief of Naval Operations in Washington, D.C. He was appointed the 26th Chief of Naval Operations in August 1996, after the death of Adm. Jeremy M. Boorda, and served until July 21, 2000.

After his retirement, Admiral Johnson was a Senior Vice President of Dominion Energy, Inc., from 2000 to 2002, and Executive Vice President from December 2002 to September 2008. Concurrently he was President and Chief Executive Officer of Dominion Delivery from 2002 to 2007, and Chief Executive Officer of Dominion Virginia Power from October 2007 to September 2008. He served as Vice Chairman of General Dynamics from September 2008 to July 2009, then becoming President and Chief Executive Officer until January 2013.

Deed of Gift

The U.S. Naval Institute is hereby authorized to make available in any format it chooses, from bound-book hard copy to electronic/digital Internet access, the audio recordings, transcripts, and videorecordings of the oral-history interview series conducted concerning the life and career of the undersigned. Disposition, repositories, and access shall be at the discretion of the Naval Institute.

The undersigned does hereby release and assign to the U.S. Naval Institute the rights and title to these interviews, with the exception that the undersigned and heirs retain the right to use the material for personal, noncommercial purposes. The copyright in the oral, transcribed, and videorecorded versions shall be held by the U.S. Naval Institute. All recordings, transcriptions, and videorecordings of the interviews shall remain the property of the U.S. Naval Institute.

Signed and sealed this 28th day of OCTOBER 2015.

Signed name [signature]

Printed name JAY L. JOHNSON

Interview Number 1 with Admiral Jay L. Johnson, USN (Ret.)

Date: 28 October 2015

James Robbins (JR): It's October 28, 2015, at 1:19, 1319. This is Dr. James Robbins, and we are starting the USNI Oral History Project interview with Admiral Jay L. Johnson, former CNO.

Thank you for agreeing to be part of this project.

Jay Johnson (JJ): You bet. My pleasure.

JR: And as I said before, at your change of command in 2000, you asked, "How do you capture a whole career in ten minutes?" Now we have hours and hours. [*Laughter*] So hopefully we can do it.

JJ: You may wish it was back to the ten minutes. [*Laughter*]

JR: Let's see. Okay. So you were born June 5, 1946?

JJ: I was.

JR: In Great Falls, Montana.

JJ: Yes.

JR: Then later moved to West Salem, Wisconsin.[1]

JJ: Yeah. As it turns out, it wasn't much later, because if you ask me my memories of Montana, there are none. My dad was an aircraft mechanic, a B-24[2] mechanic, and stationed at what I believe now is Malmstrom Air Force Base.[3] Anyway, within about six months of the time I was born, he left service and went back to Wisconsin, where the Johnson family was, and so I was essentially raised in—not essentially; I was raised in West Salem, Wisconsin. But Montana was indeed my birthplace.

JR: So he was stationed there during the war. He was in the Army Air Force?

JJ: Army Air Corps.[4] The 8th I believe.[5]

JR: Yes, B-24s, that would make sense. That's fantastic. So there's a service history in your family, then.

---

1. A village (population approximately 5,008 in 2014) in La Crosse County, Wisconsin, along the La Crosse river bordering Minnesota.
2. The Consolidated B-24 Liberator was a heavy bomber introduced in 1941 that was used extensively in World War II.
3. Malmstrom Air Force Base was established in 1941 in Great Falls, Cascade County, Montana. It was originally known as Great Falls Air Force Base. It was renamed in October 1955 in honor of vice wing commander Colonel Einar Axel Malmstrom, who had died August 21, 1954, when the T-33 Shooting Star trainer he was flying crashed near the base. Colonel Malmstrom had commanded the 356th Fighter Group in the Second World War and was shot down April 24, 1944, on his 58th combat mission. He spent the remainder of the war as a POW in Stalag Luft I in Barth, Germany.
4. The United States Army Air Corps was the primary U.S. military aviation organization from July 2, 1926, to March 9, 1942. It was succeeded by the United States Army Air Forces until the formation of the United States Air Force on September 18, 1947.
5. The 8th Air Force was established January 19, 1942, and known as VIII Bomber Command until February 22, 1944. During World War II it was active in the northern part of the European theater, conducting strategic bombing missions in France, the Low Countries, and Germany.

JJ: Yes, there is indeed. He didn't make a career of it, but he was proud of his service, as he should have been.

JR: Were there any others of your ancestors who served?

JJ: Yeah. I mean, most all of them put in their service, and I had a cousin who went to West Point[6] back in the fifties, I would say, and that sort of piqued my initial interest in the service academies.

JR: Fantastic. Before we get to your Annapolis[7] career, I saw you were an Eagle Scout.[8]

JJ: I'm an Eagle Scout. I'm a Distinguished Eagle Scout and very proud of it.

JR: You received the Distinguished Eagle Scout Award.[9]

JJ: Yeah.

JR: How did Scouting affect your life?

---

6. The United States Military Academy at West Point, New York.
7. The United States Naval Academy at Annapolis, Maryland.
8. Eagle Scout is the highest rank attainable in the Boy Scouts of America (BSA). The award dates back to 1911 and is earned by approximately 4 percent of scouts.
9. The Distinguished Eagle Scout Award is given by the National Eagle Scout Association in recognition of Eagle Scouts who have "received extraordinary national-level recognition, fame, or eminence in their field, and have a strong record of voluntary service to their community" (National Eagle Scout Association).

JJ: Well, I'll tell you a story that really will affirm that Scouting had a most profound effect on my life in many ways, but I'll get to the specific point in just a second. This town where I grew up, when I left to go to the Naval Academy, the little sign on the entry to the town said, "West Salem, Population: 1,376." So it's not a huge place. I think they probably clawed their way up to 4,500 or maybe even 5,000 lo these many years later. But the point is, it was a small town, very family-centric, and Scouting was a big part of our youth and we loved it. It taught us a lot about ourselves and about all the good things that Scouting does for you.

So in 1960, there was a National Jamboree[10] held in what's now the Black Forest, in Colorado Springs, Colorado, and our troop from West Salem, Wisconsin, a number of us were lucky enough to go to that Jamboree, and we actually took buses across Wisconsin, drove through the Badlands[11] and saw Mount Rushmore[12] and did all those things, down into Colorado, and had this great experience. For a little small-town kid, it was a big deal and really a memorable one. President Eisenhower[13] came, Roy Rogers & Sons of the Pioneers.[14] [*Laughter*] You know what I mean? Those were all big in the day.

---

10. The Boy Scout National Jamboree is a quadrennial gathering of scouts from across the country for a week of camping and other youth activities. The 1960 Jamboree at Colorado Springs, held July 22–28, celebrated the fiftieth anniversary golden jubilee of Scouting. The jamboree motto was "For God and Country."
11. The Badlands are a rugged and picturesque area of southwestern South Dakota noted for its unusual rock formations and unspoiled prairie lands. The Lakota Sioux called the area "Mako Sica," which means "land bad."
12. Mount Rushmore National Memorial is a sculpture of four U.S. presidents (George Washington, Thomas Jefferson, Theodore Roosevelt, and Abraham Lincoln) carved on Mt. Rushmore in the Black Hills region of South Dakota. It was sculpted by Gutson Borglum and his son Lincoln from 1927 to 1941.
13. Dwight D. Eisenhower (1890–1969), 34th president of the United States (1953–1961), and former Supreme Commander of the Allied Expeditionary Forces in Europe during World War II.
14. Roy Rogers (1911–1998), aka Leonard Franklin Slye, was an American western musician, radio, television, and film star. The Sons of the Pioneers was Rogers' original singing group, founded in 1934 by Rogers and his friends Bob Nolan and Tim Spencer.

But the story I was getting to is this. The Black Forest, if you're not familiar with Colorado Springs, is right across from what's now Interstate 25 north-south up to Denver and south to Pueblo, from the Air Force Academy, and the Air Force Academy in 1960 was like one year old.[15] So as part of our visit there, we were given a tour of the Air Force Academy, and as part of that tour, one of the things that happened was the Air Force Thunderbirds[16] performed, and when I saw the Thunderbirds, I said, *"That's* what I want to do."

And so time passes, I go back to Wisconsin. I graduated from high school in 1964. When it came time to apply for college and all of that, I said, "I want to go to the Air Force Academy, because I saw those guys fly. I want to fly those airplanes."

Long story short, I applied to the Air Force Academy, didn't get in. Got, I think, a first alternate appointment to the Naval Academy, and the guy who was the principal—that may not be the right word, but anyway, the guy who got the appointment I'd actually played basketball against, and he was just a jock of first proportion, you know, and a really good guy. I said, "Well, game over." He got hurt, as I recall, and fell out of the queue, and there I was. So I said, "Naval Academy? They fly the same airplanes. They do it off of carriers." And I said, this is good.

The big point of the story is, my Boy Scout trip to Colorado Springs had a very formative effect on the rest of my life.

JR: That's fantastic.

---

15. The United States Air Force Academy was founded in 1954. The Colorado Springs campus was not in use until August 1958, and the first USAFA class graduated June 3, 1959.
16. The Thunderbirds are the U.S. Air Force demonstration and aerobatic squadron, founded in 1953 and based at Nellis Air Force Base, Nevada. In 1960, the Thunderbirds flews the F-100C Super Sabre.

JJ: Yeah. And to this day, it's so funny, we have a place in Colorado Springs, so I've been going there since the sixties. And a friend of mine out there, who is a 1968 Air Force Academy graduate, as I'm a '68 Annapolis graduate, is a wonderful guy, a retired Air Force colonel named Dick Covey, an astronaut.[17] So Dick and I are playing golf one day, talking about things, and it's the small-world concept. He said, "How'd you get hooked up out here?" And I told him about the Jamboree. He said, "I was at that Jamboree." [*Laughter*] He was from I believe Florida or Alabama at the time. So here two guys, lo those many years later, compare notes about the Jamboree.

I said, "I wonder where exactly," because it's grown up so much out there, "where exactly was the Jamboree."

So he goes home. Next day I get an email. "Hey, there's actually a monument out at Briargate," which is where it was, "on our Jamboree." And I'd driven by that thing probably fifty times and never knew it was there. So that afternoon I went out and saw it, my wife took pictures. It's really cool, and it commemorates that Jamboree in 1960.

JR: Wow.

JJ: Yeah. Anyway—

---

17. Richard O. Covey (b. 1946) is a retired U.S. Air Force colonel who piloted the space shuttle *Discovery* on two missions in the 1980s and commanded the shuttles *Atlantis* and *Endeavour* in separate missions in the 1990s. He is a former test pilot and operational fighter pilot with 339 combat missions in southeast Asia. He is a 1968 graduate of the U.S. Air Force Academy.

JR: That's fantastic. That's a very good story. So, really, when we talk about your service career, it was a means to be an aviator. So aviation was really—

JJ: That's what started me, yes.

JR: Your driving spirit.

JJ: Yes, yes, yes. And there was another guy from my home town in West Salem—just passed away last year, regrettably—a wonderful man named Peter Walberg,[18] really smart, wicked smart, and Peter got an appointment to the Naval Academy two years ahead of me, and that furthered my interest. He went into the nuclear power program and didn't spend a career, but gave great service and then ended up, I think, working in the utility space as a nuke for the rest of his outside career.

JR: So you had all three academies giving you impressions, in some way, this was something to do.

JJ: Yes.

JR: Navy was smart enough to take you. [Laughs]

JJ: Well, I don't know, but yeah, I ended up at Navy and I'm really glad I did.

---

18. Peter Elon Walberg (1944–2015) graduated from West Salem High School in 1962 and from the U.S. Naval Academy in 1966. He served for ten years in the U.S. Navy Submarine Service, after which he was an engineer for Illinois Power at the Clinton nuclear power station from 1976 to 2000.

JR: That's fantastic. My dad was a pilot, too, by the way. So you were in the class of '68, entering in 1964.

JJ: Yes.

JR: What did you think? What were your first impressions when you arrived at Annapolis?

JJ: Well, when I went to Annapolis, I'd never been in an airplane before. Got in, as I recall, like a commercial DC-3[19] in La Crosse, Wisconsin, and flew, I guess, to Chicago and then out. But at any rate, the whole experience was pretty eye-watering for me, but it was okay. I liked the Naval Academy, it was hard work, but it was also a great opportunity to build lifelong bonds with lots of men—it was all men in those days—and I treasure that.

JR: How was it different then? We're talking about the mid-sixties.

JJ: Well, there was a lot going on. Vietnam[20] was going on, and I think a lot of us were very anxious to graduate so we could go help, and most of us did in one form or another.

---

19. The Douglas DC-3 was introduced as a passenger aircraft in 1936 and was widely used into the 1970s. The military variant, the C-47 Dakota, was the workhorse of U.S. air transport during World War II.
20 The Vietnam War (1955–1975). U.S. involvement in South Vietnam was escalating in this period up through 1968.

JR: Were you exposed to the war in your classes or with guest speakers or rotating faculty?

JJ: I'm sure we were, but honestly, it's not imprinted in my head that that was—I guess it probably was, from faculty and others and the news, what was going on. But we'd hear about graduates who were over there, carrier aviators were my particular interest, or Marines who were doing heroic things, that feedback would come to us and it helped affirm the rightness of what we were doing and give us incentive to move forward so we could go help these guys.

JR: How about the academy life? What was it like to you?

JJ: I liked it. What does that mean? Academy life, to me, was a great disciplinarian, and as I looked over my shoulder at that time in my life, I needed that. There was a time in high school, right before I went to Colorado, when I thought I wanted to go to the University of Wisconsin and be a doctor. It's 90 miles away, it's really cool, they've got all these fraternities, and a doctor's got to be a really good thing. And my mother, I think, had a tremendous influence on me recalibrating away from that, and then this experience at Colorado, and that just took University of Wisconsin right out of my scan pattern. [*Laughter*]

But I do believe at that time in my life, the discipline and the intensity and the focus, if you will, necessary focus, at the Naval Academy was probably the best thing that ever happened to me. I wasn't a bad kid, but I just think at that time in my life I needed that focus.

JR: It sharpened you.

JJ: Yes, yes.

JR: Were you in athletics?

JJ: I didn't play any varsity. I was in athletics in high school and I was in non-varsity athletics at the Naval Academy. My plebe year, I really hurt my knee squaring corner, actually. Bottom half goes straight ahead, top half goes 90 degrees to port, and I had to have my knee operated on plebe year, which set me back a little bit. Had four more after that. So I played athletics, but I wasn't a varsity athlete there.

JR: Most of the time when you were there, the commandant of midshipmen[21] was Sheldon Kinney.[22]

JJ: Yeah.

---

21. The commandant of midshipmen is the second in command at the Naval Academy and responsible for the day-to day-activities of the midshipmen. The commandant typically holds the rank of Navy captain or Marine colonel.

22. Sheldon Hoard Kinney (1918–2004) was a Navy rear admiral who served in World War II, the Korean War, and Vietnam. He was a former enlisted sailor who attended the U.S. Naval Academy 1937 to 1941. He received the Navy Cross for an action while commanding the destroyer USS *Bronstein* in 1943 in which he sank three German submarines and disabled a fourth in the course of one night. He also received the Navy and Marine Corps Medal for Heroism for diving into the ocean to save two downed aviators. He served as commandant of midshipmen 1963–1967.

JR: Do you have any impressions of him or stories of him?

JJ: Sheldon Kinney was a great American and a wonderful man, and he looked the part: ramrod straight, wavy gray hair, piercing eyes, squared away to a fare-thee-well. That's my memory of Admiral Kinney. But he also, if memory serves, was a heroic commander of one of the destroyer escorts. He may have even had a squadron of them. I can't recall. They were the little boats—"little boats"—little ships that did so much great work escorting in the Atlantic during the war, and Sheldon Kinney was right in the thick of that, as I recall. So he was a very seasoned combat veteran and, like I say, a great example to all of us. Admiral Kinney was really something.

JR: Inspirational guy.

JJ: Yes, very much so.

JR: He sank three German subs and disabled a fourth in one night.

JJ: Yeah.

JR: That was his Navy Cross.

JJ: Navy Cross winner, yeah.

JR: Who else was really influential among the faculty or officers?

JJ: I think Admiral Draper Kauffman,[23] who was the superintendent. He was, if not the founder, one of the earliest underwater demolition SEAL predecessors in the Navy, which is quite remarkable because he—I remember this—he had *really* bad vision. But he, too, was a remarkable guy. And Admiral Jim Calvert,[24] I think, came after him, as I recall, ex-submariner, *Nautilus*. Anyway, some good role models.

Company officers, John Kelly [phonetic], Lieutenant Commander Kelly,[25] class of '62, was one of my company officers, great guy, good friend forever, great example for all of us. So we had lots of role models. Lieutenant Colonel Cosgrove was our battalion officer for part of my time there, Bill Cosgrove, Naval Academy class of '45, still going strong, God bless him, set a great example. He is a wonderful man and a great leader. So, lots of good examples.

JR: That's good. And how about your classmates? A lot of distinguished guys came out of your class.

---

23. Rear Admiral Draper Laurence Kauffman graduated from the U.S. Naval Academy in 1933 but was not commissioned due to poor eyesight. After the outbreak of World War II in Europe he served in the British Royal Navy Volunteer Reserve, and in 1941 was commissioned in the U.S. Naval Reserve. In 1943 he organized the first U.S. Navy underwater demolition teams, the forerunner of the Navy SEALs. From 1965 to 1968 he served as the 44th superintendent of the U.S. Naval Academy.
24. Vice Admiral James Francis Calvert (1920–2009) was a 1942 graduate of the U.S. Naval Academy. He was a decorated submarine officer in World War II and continued in submarine service in the 1950s. In 1968 he became the 45th superintendent of the U.S. Naval Academy.
25. John Patrick Kelly, USNA 1962.

JJ: Mike Mullen,[26] a dear friend and a really great officer. Denny Blair.[27] Just talking about the four-stars, Mullen, Blair, Mike Hagee,[28] and, of course, we've got Jim Webb,[29] we've got Ollie North.[30]

JR: It's quite a class.

JJ: Yes, it is. But lots of flag officers at three-star grade, four-star grade, one through four. I've got classmates that if I start naming them, I'll forget somebody, so I probably shouldn't beyond Mullen and Blair, but I do know Willy Moore[31] was a company mate of mine, retired as a three-star aviator, superb. A number of them. Paul Gaffney,[32] three-star, in my company. Jay Cohen's[33] another great, ran the Office of Naval Research, two-star nuke submariner. So we have a very proud and a very giving class. Our class gave a lot to the country and continues to do so. I'm very proud of it.

---

26. Admiral (ret) Michael Glenn Mullen (b. 1946) served as the 17th chairman of the Joint Chiefs of Staff from October 1, 2007, to September 30, 2011.
27. Admiral (ret) Dennis C. Blair (b. 1947) served as the United States director of national intelligence 2009–2010.
28. General (ret) Michael William Hagee, USMC (b. 1944) was the 33rd commandant of the United States Marine Corps 2003–2006.
29. James H. Webb Jr. (b. 1946) served in the Marine Corps 1968–1972, rising to the rank of captain, and was awarded the Navy Cross for heroism in Vietnam. He served as Secretary of the Navy 1987–1988, and U.S. senator from Virginia 2007–2013. He is also a best-selling author and Emmy award–winning filmmaker.
30. Oliver L. North (b. 1943) served in the Marine Corps 1968–1990, retiring at the rank of lieutenant colonel. He was awarded the Silver Star for heroism in Vietnam. North served on the National Security Council Staff during the Reagan administration, where he was embroiled in the Iran-Contra affair scandal. After his retirement he became a best-selling author and radio and television commentator.
31. Vice Admiral (ret) Charles W. "Willy" Moore Jr. (b 1946) was a naval flight officer and deputy chief of naval operations for fleet readiness and logistics, who served as acting 58th superintendent of the United States Naval Academy June to August 2003.
32. Vice Admiral (ret) Paul G. Gaffney II (b. 1946) served as president of the National Defense University 2000–2003. After retirement he became president of Monmouth University in West Long Branch, New Jersey, from 2003 to 2013.
33. Rear Admiral (ret) Jay Martin Cohen (b. 1946) commanded the Office of Naval Research 2000–2006 and served as under secretary of homeland security for science and technology 2006–2009.

JR: Admiral Gaffney was at NDU, because I worked for him at NDU.

JJ: Mm-hmm. Then he went to Monmouth University and I think he retired from there, I believe, last year. Good man.

JR: Great guy. I enjoyed working for him.

JJ: He's terrific.

JR: Yes. So any more comments? We can dwell on your academy experience, but comparing the academy then to now, I know there have been changes, like having women at the academy and things like that, but, you know—

JJ: The midshipmen look a lot younger now. [*Laughter*]

JR: Funny how that works, isn't it?

JJ: Yeah. I'm on the foundation board, as you probably know, and so I do have occasion to get back to the academy, and it's just really gratifying and reaffirming, the rightness of that place and what they're doing. The demographic is not what I'm talking about. I'm talking about just the—when you talk to a midshipman today, you go, "That is an impressive midshipman." Male or female, it doesn't matter, okay? They're really smart, they're wicked focused, and doing great things. It's so nice to see. And it's not surprising, but it doesn't just happen, you know.

JR: Sure.

JJ: The academy works very hard to build leaders and disperse them throughout the world, in the military and in business and other places. So I'm very, very proud of the academy. I used to tell the midshipmen when I was the CNO,[34] I'd go back there to give speeches, and I'd say, "You know, I know what you're thinking. I know what you're thinking down there. 'Who is this old fart, and how long do I have to sit here?'" But then I'd say, "You know, I can remember sitting where you are as though it were yesterday." In those days it was like 30-plus years ago.

And I said, "Here's the deal, and the moral to my story to you is that you have no idea on the front end, where you are now, how fast thirty years will pass. No idea. You think you do. Trust me, you don't. But I will tell you, on the back end of that, where I am now, that it's the blink of an eye. Why am I telling you this? I'm telling you this because my message to you is don't waste a minute of it, okay? Don't waste a minute of it, because it's your life and it passes much more rapidly than you would think. So your chance to make an imprint, whatever you do, wherever you go, is, in the grand scheme of things, relatively fleeting, so don't miss a moment of it." That was my story.

JR: That's great. So you're proud of the academy. There's been a continuity of mission, spirit.

---

34. Chief of Naval Operations.

JJ: Absolutely, yes.

JR: From your day to now, they've kept it going.

JJ: Yes.

JR: Very good.

JJ: And I like to think of it as not only have they kept it going, but also they've been improving it, as it goes, and I think it's pretty obvious when you go over there and just hang around, talk to midshipmen, talk to company officers, talk to the superintendent over there, Admiral Carter[35] right now, talk to previous superintendents, like Vice Admiral John Ryan,[36] who's the chairman of the foundation right now, you'll see what that place is really made of.

JR: That's good. So you left in '68, you went to flight training after that. Any impressions of flight training? Did you do any preparatory stuff before, summer programs or anything, where you'd go and get ready?

---

35. Vice Admiral Walter E. "Ted" Carter Jr. (b. 1959) became the 62nd superintendent of the United States Naval Academy in 2014. Carter served as the 54th president of the U.S. Naval War College 2013–2014. He is a 1981 graduate of the Naval Academy and a naval flight officer.
36. Vice Admiral (ret) John R. Ryan (b. 1945) served as the 56th superintendent of the United States Naval Academy 1998–2002, and as the chancellor of the State University of New York 2005–2007.

JJ: Yes, a couple of things. One of the summers I had an opportunity to go to Patuxent River[37] and actually fly. I wanted to fly in the Phantom, F-4,[38] because that was really—

JR: It was the hot rod of the day.

JJ: The hot rod, yeah. And I ended up flying in an A-6,[39] which was pretty neat, too, and of course, I'd never been in a tactical airplane before in my life. So I flew in an OV-10[40] and an A-6 there, and as I recall, I think I flew with "Buzz" Osley [phonetic], who was class of '60 or '61. Anyway, that was a great experience.

JR: Your first time—

JJ: First time in a military jet, sucking oxygen. It was great.

JR: What year was that?

JJ: Probably '66, maybe, '65 or '66. Then I went on my first-class cruise. I wanted to go to Vietnam. I wanted to go to the carrier on Yankee Station[41] and really see what naval aviation was doing. I didn't get assigned to the carrier, but I got assigned to the destroyer

---

37. Naval Air Station Patuxent River, St. Mary's County, Maryland.
38. The McDonnell Douglas F-4 Phantom II was a two-seat, long-range supersonic fighter-bomber that entered service with the Navy in 1960 and was retired from combat use in 1996.
39. The Grumman A-6 Intruder was a twin jet, all-weather/night attack aircraft that saw service with the Navy and Marine Corps 1963–1997.
40. The North American Rockwell OV-10 Bronco was a turboprop light attack and observation aircraft that saw service 1965–1995. Its primary mission was forward air control (FAC).
41. Yankee Station was a location in the Gulf of Tonkin off the coast of South Vietnam east of Danang used by Task Force 77 to launch carrier strikes in the Vietnam War.

that was plane guard for the carriers out there, USS *Bausell*.[42] So I got to watch it all, and most of that was good, some of it was horrifying because we actually were there when the *Forrestal* blew up.[43] The *Forrestal* fire was there. Anyway, it furthered my interest in naval aviation, let's put it that way.

JR: How close were you guys to the *Forrestal*?

JJ: Well, we got very close to it because the ship helped with some of the logistics aftermath of that fire, but it was pretty amazing to watch. Scary, horrible. They did a great job saving that ship.

JR: That's quite an experience for a young guy.

JJ: Yeah. But then I saw my first experience in Asia in WestPac,[44] so it was very, very important to me and I'm glad I got to see it before I went back to really see it. [*Laughter*]

JR: No kidding. So none of this turned you off to aviation in any way.

JJ: Nuh-uh.

---

42. USS *Bausell* (DD 845) was a Gearing-class destroyer in the United States Navy during the Korean War and the Vietnam War. The ship was named for Corporal Lewis K. Bausell, USMC (1924–1944), who was awarded the Medal of Honor posthumously for "conspicuous gallantry" during the Battle of Peleliu.
43. USS *Forrestal* (CV 59) was a supercarrier named after the first secretary of defense, James Forrestal. On July 29, 1967, while on duty off the coast of South Vietnam, an accident on the flight deck resulted in a serious fire that killed 134, injured 161, and destroyed 21 aircraft.
44. Western Pacific.

JR: Then you went to flight school. Where'd you go to flight training?

JJ: Pensacola[45] first, then Meridian, Mississippi,[46] then back to Pensacola for carrier qualification in the T-2,[47] and then to Kingsville, Texas,[48] for advanced jet training. I got my wings in Corpus Christi[49] in—I think it was October of '69.

JR: So the whole process was a little over a year, year and a quarter or so.

JJ: Yeah.

JR: What were your impressions of flight school and the guys who were there? Did many guys wash out of that?

JJ: Yeah, more than a few, but plenty of them made it through, and it was really good. I loved learning how to fly, and I had some good instructors. My primary flight instructor—in those days we considered him a really old guy; I don't know how old he was, probably in his forties—was named "Swede" Froaker [phonetic], and he was a master. He had 15,000 hours, maybe 20,000. I don't know. But he also knew how to take these kids like me and teach us how to fly. It was really cool. [*Laughter*]

---

45. Naval Air Station Pensacola, Escambia County, Florida.
46. Naval Air Station Meridian, Lauderdale and Kemper Counties, Mississippi.
47. The North American T-2 Buckeye was the United States Navy's intermediate training aircraft 1959–2008.
48. Naval Air Station Kingsville, located three miles east of Kingsville, Texas.
49. Naval Air Station Corpus Christi, Nueces County, Texas.

And then the jet instructors, they were kind of like, "Wow! These guys really know how to do this, and they're trying to teach me." So it was a great experience. I loved it.

JR: Any of your classmates that you remember from then, folks you had met in flight school?

JJ: Yeah. I'll tell you one. You may know him. You know the author Steve Coonts?[50]

JR: Yeah.

JJ: *Flight of the Intruder*.

JR: Sure.

JJ: Steve and I went to flight training together.

JR: No kidding.

JJ: This is another sea story. So we go to flight training together. He goes off to A-6s, I go off to fly F-8s.[51] We both end up over in the Gulf together. He was on *Enterprise*,[52] as

---

50. Stephen Coonts (b. 1946) is a best-selling novelist who served in the Navy 1968–1977. He flew the A-6 Intruder during the Vietnam War and was awarded the Distinguished Flying Cross.
51. The Vought F-8 Crusader was a single-engine, supersonic, carrier-based air superiority aircraft that saw service principally 1957–1976.

I recall, and I was on *Oriskany*.[53] We don't see each other; life goes on. He ends up staying in the Navy for a tour as a shooter on the *Nimitz*,[54] as I recall, gets out as a lieutenant commander. I, obviously, stay in the Navy. He becomes a lawyer and then an incredible best-selling author.

So in the small-world concept again, we're out at the Broadmoor[55] and I see this Saturday Lecture Series, and the guy who's giving the lecture is this fellow name Steven P. Coonts. I told my wife, I said, "We've got to go. I haven't seen Steve Coonts since flight training."

He gave a marvelous presentation about being an author and tying it back to Vietnam and all this. He's a great storyteller in addition to being a great author. So after it was over, I went up and reintroduced myself, and now the Coontses and the Johnsons are fast friends. We both have places out there—they live in Colorado Springs. So that was a lifelong bond that went dormant for a while as we each went our own way. Now we've reconnected and we're tighter than ever.

JR: That's fantastic.

JJ: Yeah. If you really want to read a good book, try his one book, I think his only book of nonfiction. (I just read his next book; I'm under a cone of silence, but it's going to be fantastic.) His nonfiction book is called *Cannibal Queen,* and it's the story of him and his

---

52. USS *Enterprise* (CVN 65) was the world's first nuclear-powered aircraft carrier and saw service 1962–2012.
53. USS *Oriskany* (CV/CVA 34) saw service 1950–1976. The ship was named for the 1777 Battle of Oriskany during the Revolutionary War. *Oriskany* was sunk May 17, 2006, as part of a program to create artificial reefs in the Gulf of Mexico.
54. USS Nimitz (CVN 68) is a supercarrier launched in 1972 and commissioned in 1975. The ship is named for World War II Pacific fleet commander Chester W. Nimitz (1885–1966).
55. The Broadmoor is a resort hotel on Cheyenne Lake in Colorado Springs, Colorado.

son for part of it, but mostly Steve flying to all 48 states in his own Stearman biplane named *Cannibal Queen.* It's an amazing story of America, because he goes to these little airports and he meets America in every single continental state.

JR: Wow.

JJ: It's really, really a great book. And he ties part of it back to flying. If you're an aviator, it's fantastic, because he's flying this little Stearman, but he ties thoughts and memories back to Vietnam when he was flying A-6s. I love the book.

JR: That sounds fantastic. I grew up in an aviation family. It's the kind of book I want to read. Great. Well, thank you.

So I have your first tour on *Oriskany,* as you mentioned.

JJ: Hellcats, VF-191, Fighter Squadron 191.

JR: What years were you with that squadron?

JJ: Seventy-one to '73, as I recall.

JR: So those were combat cruises on station?

JJ: Two combat cruises to Vietnam, yes.

JR: And the F-8J Crusader. How was that as an aircraft?

JJ: It was a handful, but it was a great aircraft. Still trying to figure out if the wing went up or the fuselage went down, but that's an inside story. F-8 was a great airplane, the "Last of the Gunfighters,"[56] they called it, single seat, all by yourself, even on your first hop. I'm really glad I got to fly the Crusader. Everybody wanted to fly Phantoms, and the Phantom's a great airplane. I got Crusaders and I'm really glad I did. I loved it. It's a hard airplane to bring aboard the ship, but it was great.

JR: What type of missions were you flying?

JJ: We did a little bit of everything, and toward the end we were dropping bombs even from the F-8s, but we bombed, we had 20-millimeter guns, so we could strafe. In earlier days they had a lot of air-to-air, and we did combat air patrol and we did photo escort and we did strike escort missions over land, with missiles, but I never encountered an air-to-air. I never encountered a MiG[57] that I could shoot down.

JR: You were getting shot at probably by missiles.

JJ: Mm-hmm.

---

56. The Crusader was the last American fighter built with guns as the primary weapon.
57. Abbreviation of Mikoyan-and-Gurevich Design Bureau, a Soviet-era and later Russian aircraft corporation. Colloquially refers to an enemy aircraft.

JR: Were you flying mainly over the north or doing missions over the south?

JJ: Depends on where the carrier was. We were up north for some, down south for some, yes, so all over. Supported Yankee Station North, Dixie Station South,[58] as I recall.

JR: That's clever. [*Laughs*] Were you flying support missions for South Vietnamese troops?

JJ: I'm sure we were at some point. I don't recall mission specifics, to be honest with you.

JR: I was thinking maybe like during the Easter Offensive[59] in '72 or any of those big pushes.

JJ: Yeah. I'd have to look, to be honest with you. We did a lot of overland ordnance work. F-8 didn't carry much ordnance, but we gave it what we had.

JR: Did many guys in your squadron take hits? Did you lose any guys?

JJ: On the ship we lost guys, yeah, absolutely. We sure did. That was part of the risk profile.

---

58. Dixie Station was a location in the South China Sea southeast of Cam Ranh Bay used for launching strikes and close air support missions in the Vietnam War.
59. The Easter Offensive was a major offensive push by the North Vietnamese People's Army of Vietnam into South Vietnam March 30 to October 22, 1972.

JR: Sure.

JJ: And that's the risk profile of a carrier aviator when you're over there or anywhere else.

JR: The war was "winding down," but it was still dangerous.

JJ: Not if somebody's shooting at you. [*Laughter*]

JR: Right. Any of your guys POWs, captured, anything like that?

JJ: We had a couple of MIAs on the ship in the air wing. I'm trying to think of POW. I just don't recall. Nobody's name jumps out at me. I remember some of the others. We lost one guy named Dan Borah, "Dazzle" Dan Borah,[60] A-7[61] pilot. He went down over land, never got him back, and I think there was speculation he may have been a POW for a while, but I don't think so, in retrospect.

JR: How was morale on your combat cruises? Were people generally positive?

JJ: Yes.

---

60. Lieutenant Daniel Vernor Borah Jr. (1946–1972), served with Attack Squadron 155 on the USS *Oriskany*. He crash landed in Quang Tri province in South Vietnam on September 24, 1972, and died in captivity soon after.
61. The Ling-Temco-Vought A-7E Corsair II was a supersonic light attack aircraft that saw service with the Navy 1967–1991.

JR: Happy to be out there doing what they were trained to do?

JJ: Yes, and we had great leadership. Commanding officer of USS *Oriskany* was one of the most impressive officers I've ever met in my life. His name was John Barrow,[62] and he was class of, I think, 1947, fighter pilot, and he was remarkable. An example. He was a leader, okay? A couple examples.

Imagine Lieutenant (junior grade) Johnson wandering back to the ready room in the bowels of the 02 deck or whatever it was on the *Oriskany,* and hearing somebody say, "Make a hole." It was the captain coming through. Captain Barrow didn't just plow through. He'd stop, he'd ask you how it's going, he'd call you by name, which to this day blows me away. I found out later he studied his air wing, because these guys were going to fight and maybe die. He'd study the pictures of the air wing and he could tie a face to a name. Remarkable, remarkable leader.

So you ask about morale. If you've got somebody like John Barrow in the lead, it's hard not to be motivated to do good things. He would also—we'd come off station to go into port, the Philippines, usually, after doing combat for, I'll say, 30 days, whatever the period of time was, and we'd usually send some airplanes ashore, work on them, whatever, mostly in the Philippines, as I said. Captain Barrow wasn't up on the bridge just minding his own business, taking care of business up there; he actually was down there on the flight deck, at the catapult, and he became the catapult officer. He would take

---

62. Rear Admiral John Curtis Barrow (1926–1987) commanded the USS *Oriskany* 1970–1972. He was a 1949 graduate of the U.S. Naval Academy and retired as assistant deputy chief of Naval Operations for plans, policy, and operations. His decorations included the Distinguished Flying Cross.

your salute when you said, "I'm ready to fire off the boat." He would take the salute and launch you off the ship.

JR: No kidding.

JJ: Yeah. Amazing, man. I loved John Barrow. He was remarkable. He made one of the strongest impressions on me of any leader I've ever met in my life. I said, "*That* is a leader." Yeah, great guy, and he looked the part, too, just like Sheldon Kinney did. He looked like a—

JR: Ramrod straight.

JJ: Ramrod straight, good-looking fighter pilot, carrier XO extraordinaire, and a quality human being of the first order, yeah.

JR: So these officers of integrity were important in sort of—

JJ: You bet.

JR: —being an example for your own career development.

JJ: Yes, sure. Yeah, yeah. He was quite a guy.

JR: Did you ever run into him later and get a chance to tell him?

JJ: I did, in fact. He ended up—"ended up." He had a tour of duty, as I recall, at Oceana,[63] at Virginia Beach. He was the admiral there for a while. Yeah, I got to see him then and talk to him, and he died some years later, before his time. But anyway, great man, great family, privileged to know him.

JR: Did you see anything about—well, I guess you had ended that tour in the *Oriskany* before the fall of Saigon, or see any of that. I don't know if you were later around for the boat people or any of those experiences.

JJ: Not directly, that I recall. I can't remember the date we left. I could check my aircraft logbooks, except they're [unclear]. [*Laughter*]

JR: Yeah, that would have been two years later. I was just wondering if on subsequent tours you might have seen something along that line.

JJ: I do remember, though, I'll tell you one other—how the world turns. So my next tour of duty's in Washington, D.C., at the Bureau of Naval Personnel. I lived in a townhouse out in Burke, Virginia, and there was a new mall being put in right there next to our townhouses, called Rolling Valley Mall. I have no idea if it's still named that, but that's what it was then, in '73 or '74. And I went into this pizza place one night and ordered a pizza. The guy who was running it, they looked like Vietnamese. Long story short, the

---

63. Naval Air Station Oceana located in Virginia Beach, Virginia.

guy who was the owner, as it turns out, comes over and strikes up a conversation. I guess he recognized my haircut. Turns out he was the chief of police. You know the Pulitzer—

JR: General Loan.[64]

JJ: Yeah.

JR: I know that story. I wrote a book about it. [*Laughs*]

JJ: That's the guy, right?

JR: Yeah. He had the pizza place.[65]

JJ: Yeah. And he said, "See that guy who's cooking your pizza? He was the F-5 commander at Danang."

JR: No kidding.

JJ: Yeah. [*Laughs*]

---

64. General Nguyễn Ngọc Loan (1930–1998), chief of national police for the Republic of South Vietnam. He was pictured in Eddie Adam's Pulitzer Prize–winning 1968 photograph "Saigon Execution" executing Viet Cong terrorist Nguyễn Văn Lém.
65. Le Trois Continents, Burke, Virginia.

JR: Well, General Loan, before he was the head of security in Saigon, he was a pilot. He was the first southerner to bomb the North in the South Vietnamese Air Force.

JJ: Yes. And I remember reading his obituary and looking at what he and his family had done, in terms of coming here and making a life, and it was listing what his children had done, and they were all doctors or lawyers. It was just a remarkable story to me, very impressive.

JR: In general, the story of the South Vietnamese who came here is just amazing.

JJ: Yeah.

JR: And not to go too off topic, but I was at a thing—I got to know folks when I was writing about him and about the Tet Offensive, which was my topic. I'll bring you a copy of that next time. And so I got invited to some of these South Vietnamese expatriate events where they would get together—

JJ: Wow.

JR: And they had these amazing American families of folks with just all of the things that they've done. Someone told me—this may be apocryphal, but they said if you add up the GDP of all the expatriates in America, it's bigger than Vietnam, post-communist. So I kind of believe it.

JJ: Yeah, yeah. He was quite a guy.

JR: Yeah. Well, I'll bring you that thing. There's also a documentary about him that just came out.

JJ: Is that right?

JR: Yeah, about the photo and Eddie Adams, who took it, and General Loan and the guy he shot, who was a real bastard, a very bad guy.

JJ: Yeah.

JR: His name was Bay Lop, very bad. But anyway, it's called *Eddie Adams: Saigon '68*. It's just a short film. Now they're trying to make it into a bigger thing. It won some kind of award and stuff. Anyway, the truth's getting out about General Loan. [*Laughs*]

JJ: Yeah, yeah.

JR: That's interesting that you went to his pizza place.
    So, after BuPers,66 I don't guess there was any kind of interesting story out of that experience. Or maybe there was.

---

66. Bureau of Naval Personnel.

JJ: No, I mean, I learned a lot, moving naval officers around. It was a good experience. I liked my time at Bureau of Naval Personnel so well I ended up doing three tours there.

JR: Was that inside the Building[67] or at the Navy Yard?[68]

JJ: No.

JR: Where was it?

JJ: The Bureau of Naval Personnel in that first instance was located in the Navy Annex,[69] which has been razed.

JR: Yeah, it's gone now.

JJ: Yeah. Seventh wing of the Navy Annex.

JR: There you go.

JJ: In fact, all three of my tours were there. I still haven't seen the plan for what they're going to do with that land, except it's going to become part of Arlington Cemetery,[70] I think.

---

67. Colloquial term for the Pentagon.
68. The Washington Navy Yard in Southeast Washington, D.C., is the oldest U.S. Navy post.
69. The Navy Annex (Federal Office Building 2) was a large office building near the Pentagon in Arlington, Virginia. It was in use from 1941 to 2013.

JR: Well, I know they're building something downhill from it, because they took out the NavEx, which was so convenient.

JJ: Yeah. Exactly.

JR: There's something going on below that parking lot for the Air Force Memorial,[71] but I don't know what it is.

JJ: Yeah.

JR: So when did you go back to sea?

JJ: Well, after the time at BuPers from, what, '73 to '75, maybe early '76, I went back to sea duty, and I had to transition because the F-8s were going or gone. That's when I transitioned to the F-14 Tomcat[72] and got my training back at Miramar, where I'd learn to fly the F-8, but the squadron that I was assigned to was in Virginia Beach at Naval Air Station Oceana.

---

70. Arlington National Cemetery is a United States military cemetery in Arlington County, Virginia, established in 1864.
71. The United States Air Force Memorial is located in Arlington, Virginia, near the Pentagon and Arlington National Cemetery. It was unveiled in 2006.
72. The Grumman F-14 Tomcat is an American supersonic, twin-engine, two-seat, variable-sweep wing fighter aircraft that saw service with the U.S. Navy 1974–2006.

JR: Was that VF-142?[73]

JJ: Mm-hmm. Ghostriders. You bet.

JR: What was your impression of the Tomcat? There are a lot of fans.

JJ: I'm one of them. [*Laughter*] Yeah, it was a great airplane, a great airplane. You had to fly the engines, but it was a great airplane.

JR: What was great about it?

JJ: Back in those days, the wing sweep, it was just awesome, and it was a great maneuvering airplane. My first experience with somebody in the backseat. Never had a backseat in an F-8. So, learning that. The systems in those days were really great. I loved flying the Tomcat, really glad I got the opportunity.

JR: So VF-142 deployed to the Mediterranean?

JJ: Mm-hmm.

JR: Were you on that deployment?

---

73. VF-142 Ghostriders was a U.S. Navy fighter squadron established on August 24, 1948, as VF-193, redesignated VF-142 on October 15, 1963. The unit was disestablished on April 30, 1995.

JJ: USS *Dwight D. Eisenhower*.[74] I think it was *Eisenhower*. May have been *Nimitz*. I can't remember. But we did go on the shakedown cruise for—maybe it was either *Ike* or *Nimitz*, and we ended up going to South America and then deployed to the Med.

JR: There was an intercept of a Soviet Bear bomber.[75] Were you around for that one?

JJ: I'd spent hours beside Bear bombers. [*Laughter*] Yeah, yeah, lots of them.

JR: What are those missions like anyway? You see them sometimes reported and there's a picture of U.S. and Soviet aircraft or something like that. How did that work?

JJ: Usually you were out at sea and there was a keep-out zone measured in hundreds of miles or whatever it was; it probably varied some from place to place. Then if we had indications that the Soviet aircraft were going to penetrate that, you didn't want them penetrating it without being escorted, so the fighter pilots stood alerts on the aircraft carriers. There were different readiness conditions, alert conditions on the carrier. And if nothing was going on, let's say maybe it was a 30-minute alert, which meant you were down in the ready room watching a movie or working with your troops or whatever you were doing, but you had to be ready to launch within thirty minutes. That went all the way up to an Alert 5 or even on the catapult, in the aircraft, strapped in, engines turning, and then depending, they'd shoot you off and it was your job then to go intercept

---

74. USS *Dwight D. Eisenhower* (CVN 69) is a Nimitz-class nuclear-powered aircraft carrier commissioned in 1977. It is named after the 34th president of the United States.
75. The Tupolev Tu-95 "Bear" is a four-engine turboprop-powered strategic bomber that entered service with the Soviet Union in 1956 and has continued to be flown by the Russian Federation.

whoever was infringing on your space and escort them. So over the years I got a lot of escort time on Bears and Badgers[76] and other things.

JR: Would you communicate with the Soviet pilots?

JJ: No, but you'd always usually have some form of communications, all the things you read about, you know, the Soviet guys holding out a *Playboy* centerfold from the inside of the airplane or whatever it was. Some of that's probably fiction. Some of it's true, where they'd hold up American flags or they'd shoot you the bird or whatever it was. But yeah, you'd get up close to those guys and you'd study the airplane, too, and take pictures of their airplane to see if there were new antennas and things like that. I wonder, as I see some of these pictures today, I'll bet those are probably some of the same Bears we escorted thirty years ago. [*Laughter*]

JR: Could be. Was it ever apparent that they were doing this more than a pro forma, like they were really pushing it, like they were really trying to make something happen, or was it just like they would do it, you would escort them, and that was it?

JJ: I never got the feeling in any of the ones I did that we were going to turn arm up and try to shoot somebody down, but you were always prepared to do that, don't get me wrong. It was serious business in those days. Still is.

---

76. The Tupolev Tu-16 "Badger" was a high-speed turbojet bomber deployed by the Soviet Union in 1954 and continuing with the Russian Federation until 1993.

JR: Sure.

JJ: But let's just say I don't recall any confrontational escorts, if that makes sense.

JR: Any contacts with Soviet ships that happened when you were out there?

JJ: I'm sure there probably were contacts with Soviet ships, [unclear], maybe. I don't know. But again, they were out there. We'd mark them. We'd track them just like they were trying to track us.

JR: Because people forget a lot of the Cold War stuff, but it's becoming increasingly relevant.

JJ: Yes, it is indeed. It sure is.

JR: So people should not forget.

JJ: Yeah.

JR: That's my editorial comment to the future. [*Laughs*]

JJ: It's a good one.

JR: Don't forget the Cold War, because it wasn't always cold. Stuff happened.

JJ: Yeah.

JR: I have you with VF-101.[77]

JJ: I was the executive officer. The Grim Reaper is the VF-101, which is "the Rag," as we called it, the training squadron that taught frontseaters and backseaters and maintainers how to take care of the Tomcat and fly it. You bet. It was a good tour. Shore duty. Great tour. Worked for a commanding officer named Bud Dougherty,[78] a good friend, a great CO.

JR: So then you were in the position of being one of the inspirational old hands at that point to these young guys.

JJ: I guess, although I didn't consider myself an old hand at that time. [*Laughter*]

JR: But they did from their perspective.

JJ: Yeah, yeah. But VF-101 was great duty, great duty.

---

77. Fighter Squadron 101 (VF-101) the "Grim Reapers" was established in 1952 and deactivated in 2005. In 2012 it was reactivated as Strike Fighter Squadron 101 (VFA-101).
78. Francis "Bud" J. Dougherty was commissioned through Officer Candidate School in Newport, Rhode Island, in December 1960. He served two combat tours in Vietnam, and was awarded the Silver Star, two Distinguished Flying Crosses, Meritorious Service medal, 14 air medals, and a Navy Commendation medal.

JR: So in this period—and we're talking now—we're getting in the late seventies, end of the draft, you know, start of the all-volunteer force, so-called hollow force, defeat in Vietnam, so called. How was it generally? What was the mood? Were guys getting out or—

JJ: I think a lot of guys were getting out, and a number of my friends, aviators, got out back in those days to fly with the airlines, a lot of them. But there was still plenty of us that were staying in who I knew, obviously. People would ask me, after I was the CNO or flag officer, "How do you set yourself up to be the CNO?" or, "How do you set yourself up to be a flag officer? Did you know you wanted to be a flag officer when you were at the Naval Academy?" Those kinds of questions.

I go, "No to all the above. No, you can't set yourself up." My view, certainly when I was flying and probably at the time of VF-101 and the war winding down, and so on, was, look, I had no intention on day one of being a career naval officer. I wanted to fly pointy-nosed airplanes off carriers. And I kind of rationalized my way into saying, as long as I'm doing that, as long as I'm hopefully making a difference and, hopefully, enjoying myself, I'm going to stay in. So I looked at the airlines once, like everybody else probably has, every pilot has. I just said, "I don't want to do that. I like what I'm doing." So I stayed. The point of that is, morale notwithstanding with people getting out and the war and all the bad karma around those of us who served over there, I still felt that we had things to do in other parts of the world and a really important mission, so I stayed with it. Never regretted it.

JR: Did you ever personally experience any anti-military feelings from folks?

JJ: Sure. When *Oriskany* would sail or come back—*Oriskany* was homeported in Alameda, Oakland, California.[79] In order to get to the pier or out of the pier to the big water, you had to go under the Golden Gate Bridge. I can remember I was shocked at first, but then I understood it, we had to cover everything, put as many airplanes as we could in the hangar bay, and protect everything on the flight deck and clear the flight deck because when we'd go under the Golden Gate Bridge, all manner of really bad stuff would fall from that bridge that people were throwing on you.

JR: No kidding.

JJ: Yeah.

JR: So hippies would be out there—

JJ: Bad stuff, yeah.

JR: That's interesting. Haven't heard that story before. That's something.

Well, I guess it's understandable that around this time, though, that you would look at the airlines or what, because people get in eight, ten years, something like that,

---

79. Naval Air Station Alameda, on San Francisco Bay, California.

they've re-upped a couple of times, then that's really your decision point of are you going to go for twenty or not.

JJ: Right.

JR: Sort of like your first decision for a career.

JJ: I got early-selected, as I recall, to lieutenant commander, and I think that helped make my decision that I might want to stay around.

JR: Were you married at this time and with kids?

JJ: I was married, with one daughter.

JR: How was family life?

JJ: Challenging. Good but challenging, you know.

JR: They were moving around with you?

JJ: Mm-hmm. Oh, yeah.

JR: What did your daughter think about that?

JJ: I think she liked it at the time. She did. My mother just couldn't understand, though. She never could understand why when Vietnam was over I still had to go on these deployments. [*Laughter*]

JR: You had to explain Navy to her. [*Laughter*]

JJ: I did, time and time again. "Oh, yes, I understand, but I still just don't like that." Anyway.

JR: You want to take a break or anything?

JJ: Sure. Let's do that.

[Begin File 2]

JR: Okay. I should probably say that we're continuing with Jim Robbins and Jay Johnson on the USNI oral history. Again, this is the second round for October 28, 2015.

You were commanding officer of VF-84?[80]

JJ: Mm-hmm.

JR: When did you start that?

---

80. Fighter Squadron 84 (VF-84) "Jolly Rogers" was established in 1955 and disestablished in 1995.

JJ: I think it was probably '83, '84, in there. The Jolly Rogers.

JR: Yeah, famous from *The Final Countdown*.[81]

JJ: Right.

JR: That was before you were there, I guess, but yeah, famous from that movie. What stood out from that period when you were in command?

JJ: Well, first command and a great squadron, flying beautifully painted black tail skull and crossbones Tomcats. [*Laughter*] It was wonderful, on board USS *Nimitz*.

JR: Where did you deploy to?

JJ: We were in the Med. Where else did we go? Mediterranean deployments. I'm trying to recall if we went—no, I don't think we went north. That came later.

JR: So what were the special challenges of commanding a squadron?

JJ: Well, it's the old "buck stops here" to a certain extent, but I would say when you're a young commanding officer, there's not much daylight, age daylight, between you and

---

81. *The Final Countdown* is a 1980 feature film starring Kirk Douglas in which the USS *Nimitz* is sent back in time to just before the December 7, 1941, attack on Pearl Harbor. VF-84 was prominently featured in the movie.

your department heads and those that you've sort of grown up with. So maintaining a relationship that is not only respectful of the rank and position but also respectful of the friendship and the professional expertise of those, a number of whom are, I'm sure, better pilots than I ever was, is—I wouldn't call it a challenge, but it's just part of the realities of being commanding officer, and I was a young commanding officer. So, earning respect and being a positive leader, this is pretty elemental stuff, but the first time down the chute, it can be challenging. And working for the air wing commander, working with the other commanding officers in the air wing, understanding the relationships within that circle, if you will, and the flag on board, the captain of the ship, so it was a tremendous learning experience that I hope imparted good things on the men—and again, at that time it was all men—of the Jolly Rogers. We had a good squadron. We were very good. And we had a good air wing. We were part of a very good air wing. So I was very proud of that time.

JR: Yeah, that's when, in your career, you're moving from a primarily tactical point of view to a broader—

JJ: Yeah, the perspective is opening. That's exactly right. And that's probably the point where you really start to appreciate the imperative to delegate and trust, and lo and behold, the commanding officer really can't do it all. You really do need the team around you to do their part and feed each other. So the delegation and trust piece becomes really important. It's always important, but I think the first time you're in a commanding officer position, you really feel that and learn it, learn why it's important, and you get to watch others senior to you and your peers as they work the same realities. So it was a good time.

JR: You said in one of your addresses that you don't tell people how to do their job; you tell them what you want and let them do their job.

JJ: Yeah, and I think the more senior you get, the more complex things get, the more true that statement becomes. He or she who tries to do it all themselves will be frustrated, pissing other people off, and sub-optimizing whatever it is you're trying to do, in my opinion. So it's a team sport and it's very serious, and everybody counts. The sooner you can understand that and then build a relationship set throughout an organization that's mutually reinforcing to that, the better off you'll be.

JR: So this was really when you were starting to develop those leadership ideas and putting into practice things you'd observed from senior leaders that you'd been around over the years or observed.

JJ: Yeah. And as is always the case, you learn some good things from senior leaders and you see some bad things from senior leaders, so you try to say—to my earlier story about Admiral Barrow, John Barrow—"I want to be just like that." And then in other cases, over the years you say, "If I ever get to that position, I'm never going to do that to my people." So that's part of life's reality, whether you're in the military, whether you're in business, whether you're just living life.

JR: Right. You can get a lesson from anything.

JJ: Exactly.

JR: So true. So you moved on to commander of Carrier Air Wing One.[82]

JJ: You bet. CAG-1.

JR: So this is when we're getting up into the scrapes with Libya.

JJ: Mm-hmm.

JR: I wanted to talk about that in some detail.

JJ: We'd done some of that. We'd had a lot of practice down there on the Gulf of Sidra[83] when I was the CO of VF-84, too, so this had been ongoing for quite some time.

JR: So you'd had encounters with the Libyans from your squadron command?

JJ: Mm-hmm. You bet.

---

82. Carrier Air Wing One is a U.S. Navy aircraft carrier air wing based at Naval Air Station Oceana, Virginia.
83. A body of water in the Mediterranean Sea on the north coast of Libya.

JR: Like what kind of things were going on?

JJ: Well, remember the famous "Line of Death"[84] down there in the Gulf of Sidra? It was freedom-of-navigation stuff. There was a lot going on. I recall days when we'd fly missions and do intercepts on Libyan Mirages[85] and actually do turns with them, knock it off and they'd go back to their base and we'd go back to the ship. My dear friend Hank Kleemann, now departed, and his backseater, Dave Venlet [phonetic], ended up shooting down two fitters [phonetic] one morning.[86] Then the whole game changed after that. [*Laughs*]

JR: Were they in your squadron or a different one?

JJ: No, the sister squadron.

JR: Although on the same ship?

JJ: Yeah.

---

84. In 1973 Libyan leader Muammar Gaddafi (1940–2011) laid claim to international waters in the Gulf of Sidra, creating a supposed "line of death" for any ships or aircraft crossing into his claimed territory.
85. Libya fielded several French Dassault Mirage aircraft, such as variants of the Mirage 5D and F1.
86. On August 19, 1981, two Libyan Su-22 Fitter aircraft fired on two American F-14 Tomcats off the Libyan coast. One of the Libyan aircraft was downed by Cdr. Henry "Hank" Kleemann and Lt. David "DJ" Venlet, the other by Lt. Lawrence "Music" Muczynski and Lt. (jg) James "Luca" Anderson. This became known as the Gulf of Sidra incident.

JR: Yeah, I remember that incident. So even a couple years before [Operation] El Dorado Canyon,[87] the Libyans were out there probing, kind of pushing you guys?

JJ: Well, I don't know that they were pushing us, but they didn't like the fact that we were there, and they declared the "Line of Death" and "Thou shall not cross the Line of Death," you know. We said, "Whatever." [*Laughs*]

JR: Would they try to harass you guys by turning on their anti-air radar and things like that?

JJ: I don't remember that, honestly. If they had it, I'm sure they probably did. Like I said, it was pretty respectful until they crossed the line and got shot down one day.

JR: Right. Then things got a little more dicey?

JJ: Well, yeah. There was more separation, shall we say.

JR: Were there incidents where they sent ships out?

JJ: Yeah. I don't recall specifics of any of that, to be honest with you, but leading up to El Dorado Canyon was very busy.

---

87. Operation El Dorado Canyon was the code name for air strikes by the United States against Libya on April 15, 1986.

JR: So you were Commander Carrier Air Wing One at that time. We're talking about March and April of '86, when ultimately there was the LaBelle disco bombing.[88]

JJ: Mm-hmm.

JR: And then the strike on Benghazi and Tripoli.

JJ: Yes.

JR: So when did the planning start for those kind of things?

JJ: I can't tell you specific—I just don't recall, but it's fair to say that with all of the things that had been going on down there from my time as commanding officer, from my time as CAG, many plans had been made, so it's not like you're cold-starting on a plan. I think there was lots of planning that had taken place over time on how to deal with different circumstances with the Libyans. At least that's my memory of it. That's not to say that wasn't the plan for El Dorado Canyon, but that, I think, started shaping after the bombing at the disco and when we committed to taking action. So that was—I can't remember the date of the bombing. Do you remember?

JR: I'm pretty sure it was April 15.

---

88. On April 5, 1986, Libyan agents bombed the La Belle discothèque in West Berlin, killing 3 and wounding 230. Two of the dead and 79 of the wounded were American servicemen. The bombing became the pretext for the Operation El Dorado Canyon raids.

JJ: Of '86.

JR: Of '86. I'll check that, but yeah, I'm pretty sure. I think the disco bombing was the 5th and then ten days later. So you guys were in the Med when the terror attack happened in Berlin. How did it—

JJ: Well, we knew that—I mean, we'd gotten orders and it was all very—well, let's just say we knew we were going to do something, so we began rehearsing. And as the thing evolved, rehearsing things like coming off the carrier at night and not climbing like you normally climb, but actually punching yourself level coming off the catapult in the dark, which is—shall we call it an unnatural experience? But you had to train yourself to do that, because it's really, really unnatural. Why? Because we wanted to stay low level so we could be beneath the radars until we all positioned ourselves wherever we were going. But things like that. So we practiced in another part of the Mediterranean where nobody knew or cared.

JR: What role did you play in putting together the attack plan?

JJ: Well, both the carriers that were there and the Sixth Fleet[89] commander, who at that time was Admiral Frank Kelso,[90] were involved in putting together our pieces of the plan and bringing it all together. It was actually, I thought, very well laid out, the Air Force up

---

89. The Sixth Fleet is the United States Navy's operational fleet and staff of United States Naval Forces Europe, headquartered at Naval Support Activity Naples, Italy.
90. Admiral Frank Benton Kelso II (1933–2013) served as 24th Chief of Naval Operations 1990–1994. He was a 1956 graduate of the U.S. Naval Academy.

north doing their part and then orchestrating their arrival with synchronizing the strikes from the carriers east and west. It was quite an operation.

JR: And even though it was joint, it was kind of separated geographically.

JJ: Yes.

JR: Since their targets were mainly in the Tripoli area and your targets were mainly Benghazi.

JJ: Well, we on *America*[91] were on the Tripoli side. *Coral Sea*[92] was on the Benghazi side. So everything our ship and air wing did was Tripoli-centric.

JR: Which targets were you hitting?

JJ: Well, our specific role where I was, was to fly air cover for the F-111s[93] that were coming in from England and radar suppressors. Missile and flag suppressors were the A-7's role in large measure on our side. So we were the structure around which the protection was set up for the arrival of the F-111s who were coming in to actually do the bombing at Tripoli.

---

91. USS *America* (CVA/CV 66) was a *Kitty Hawk*-class supercarrier commissioned in 1965 and decommissioned in 1996. In 2005 *America* was scuttled southeast of Cape Hatteras.
92. USS *Coral Sea* (CV/CVB/CVA 43) was a *Midway*-class aircraft carrier commissioned in 1947 and decommission in 1990. She was named for the 1942 Battle of the Coral Sea in World War II.
93. The General Dynamics F-111 Aardvark was a multifaceted supersonic, medium-range interdictor and tactical attack aircraft. It was also used for aerial reconnaissance and electronic-warfare missions and could be outfitted as a strategic nuclear bomber. It saw service with the U.S. Air Force 1967 to 1998.

JR: So you guys were the first ones in?

JJ: We weren't in. We were standing off and they were the first ones in on that side. But yes, in terms of the anti-radiation missiles and the things that were fired to suppress the radars before the 111s came, yes, that was our primary role.

JR: What were your impressions of that operation, how it went?

JJ: I guess, overall, it went okay. I think it was really made much more difficult when the French wouldn't let the 111s come through and they had to go all the way around and come in through Gibraltar, as I recall.[94] We lost a couple of 111s; one for sure and I think maybe two. I can't remember right now. And they did damage and put the first salvo in Gaddafi's front yard, but I think it made a hell of a statement.

JR: Was there any discussion or thought that this was going to lead to more things?

JJ: Sure. I mean, you're always planning for that, and we were prepared for that, but it didn't, as you recall, in the short term, anyway.

JR: But there were plans for more comprehensive missions if needed?

---

94. 18 F-111s of the 48th Tactical Fighter Wing and the 20th Tactical Fighter Wing participated in the mission. Their round-trip flight between RAF Lakenheath/RAF Upper Heyford, United Kingdom, and Libya of 6,400 miles took 13 hours and was the longest fighter combat mission in history.

JJ: Yes.

JR: As an important operation and being the commander of the air wing—

JJ: I thought we did a really good job.

JR: You thought your guys—

JJ: Yeah, they did a superb job and they suppressed. I'll never forget it, we were all in position and it wasn't like you had Apple watch accuracy in those days, but you were taking the time and everything was on the clock, and it was radio silence and it was three, two, one, pop. And the A-7s and the F-14 covers popped up from out over the water, and I'll never forget looking down on Tripoli and saying, "They don't have a clue that we're here."

And then the radiation, this started being fired from our guys, and then shortly thereafter, you could see the city waking up a little bit, and triple-A [anti-aircraft artillery] just being shot up at the sky, and then again, turn away, come around the corner, on the clock, three two, one, where's the F-111? And about three seconds later, we saw the bomb go off in Gaddafi's front yard; you couldn't actually see the front yard, but you saw the first set of explosions and then they came through. So it was a hell of an operation, and at the same time *Coral Sea* over on the Benghazi side, which as I recall was all Navy, did their thing, time-synchronized.

But it was a long night, refueled many times, stayed out when the 111 got shot down to try to effect some kind of a SAR,[95] to no avail, as I recall, that night. But anyway, I was really proud of the air wing, what they did, the whole team, really, battle group. We'd rehearsed it, we'd practiced it, and we executed it very well.

JR: That's great. It did have a strategic effect.

JJ: Yes.

JR: The message was sent, clearly.

JJ: Mm-hmm.

JR: What else stands out from that period of your career?

JJ: Well, that was a big deal for everybody, but it also set the plate for what came later for me and, I think, others in terms of the development of the Super CAG Program,[96] which I don't know if this is the time to talk about that or not.

JR: We can start, because we'll probably revisit, after I can look up what the transcript is and do a little more work, and we can talk more about these things. So, yeah, go ahead.

---

95. Search and rescue operation.
96. In 1983 Secretary of the Navy John Lehman elevated the commander of the air group (CAG) position to the rank of captain and made the position coequal with the captain of the aircraft carrier in which the air wing embarked. Both officers reported to the embarked flag officer who was commander of the carrier battle group. These new commands were known as "Super CAGs" during the phase-in period.

JJ: When I left that air wing job, I then went to be the operations officer for the Sixth Fleet.

JR: When about was that?

JJ: Eighty-eight? I could look on my flag transcript, which I've got somewhere. But anyway—

JR: We'll clean it up. [*Laughs*]

JJ: Yeah. I went to Sixth Fleet as ops officer as a fresh-caught captain, and that was about the time that they were screening my group for O-6 command. Of course, for an aviator that meant hopefully—a carrier aviator—either going nuclear power or going to a deep-draft and then a carrier command.

Now that I say that, I think I missed a step in there. I either went from commanding officer direct to CAG or I had another BuPers tour in there. I can't remember. I should remember.

JR: Well, unfortunately, the current bio on the Navy site only has highlights.

JJ: Yeah, but I've got it. Anyway, we'll clean that up.

JR: Yeah.

JJ: But I had another BuPers tour as a commander and then the Sixth Fleet ops job, which was great, working for Vice Admiral Ken Moranville,[97] who came after Admiral Kelso, both now deceased.

Then during that time, former secretary John Lehman[98] had put a letter in, suggesting strongly that the Navy develop this Super CAG Program, whereby we made the Air Wing Command a major command at the O-6 level instead of a bonus command at the O-5 level. So I was actually CAG-1 twice because I was one of the ones selected for the first Super CAG slots.

It was very exciting, but I actually was concerned about it for a while. I was working on my ship quals even when I was a commanding officer and before on the carrier to bring her alongside for refueling and getting by OD underway qualifications. But I'd really wanted to command a carrier, and this was new, and I guess there was a while you thought you weren't sure whether this was going to be real or just a test. But it was real. It's real to this day, and I actually think it was a brilliant John Wayne move, because he saw the complexity and the need to basically up the game for the aviation side of the air wing, for the aviation side of the battle group, which was centered on the carrier in the air wing. It was his belief that, without putting words in his mouth, both the carrier CO and the air wing commander ought to be coequal instead of one at the O-6 level and one at the O-5 level.

---

97. Vice Admiral Kendall E. Moranville (1932–2001) entered the Naval Air Cadet Program in 1953 and received his wings in 1954. He served two tours of duty in Vietnam and at the time of his retirement in 1988 was commander of the U.S. Navy Sixth Fleet.
98. John Francis Lehman Jr. (b. 1942) served as Secretary of the Navy in the Reagan administration, 1981–1987.

JR: Right.

JJ: So there were five or six of us who had been CAGs, and I think been in Libya, in my case, El Dorado Canyon, and in the case of the CAG on the *Coral Sea,* and two or three others, and then several of us got selected for Super CAG out of that. So that was our major command, and when you'd finished that command, then you were eligible for flag.

JR: So that would be talking '89, '90, in there?

JJ: Thereabouts, yeah.

JR: When did you pin on a one-star?

JJ: I think I got selected in '90. I think that's right. I went to the Naval War College[99] to be a part of the CNO's Strategic Studies Group.[100]

Let's pause.

[Begin File 3]

JR: Okay, we're rolling again.

---

99. The U.S. Naval War College, founded in 1884, is located in Newport, Rhode Island.
100. The Chief of Naval Operations Strategic Studies Group (SSG) was established by Chief of Naval Operations Admiral Thomas B. Hayward in 1981 with the mission to "generate revolutionary naval warfare concepts."

JJ: So, CO Fighter Squadron 84 from October '81 to January '83; then back to BuPers as head of the Aviation Junior Officer Assignment Branch from '83 to October '84; then CAG-1, March '85 to July '86, that's El Dorado Canyon; then Sixth Fleet ops as a fresh-caught captain from July of '86 to June of '87; Carrier Air Wing One Super CAG from February of '88 to July of '89. And then, as I said, Naval War College as a Strategic Studies Group fellow from '89 to '90, and that's when I made flag. Then went back to BuPers as a one-star to be the head of distribution detailing, as they call it, Pers-4.

JR: What was your experience at Naval War College?

JJ: It was a good one. I don't know if you're familiar with the Strategic Studies Group.

JR: Nuh-uh.

JJ: That was a group of O-6-level officers from all warfare specialties, Marine officers, later they brought in Coast Guard officers, and they were under the tutelage of a senior seasoned person. In my time, it was Robin Pirie,[101] who was class of '55 Naval Academy. I don't know if you know Robin, but a terrific guy. He'd been around the Navy and military. His father was a retired three-star, Vice Admiral Robert B. Pirie,[102]

---

101. Robert B. Pirie Jr. (b. 1933) was a 1955 graduate of the U.S. Naval Academy. He retired as a captain in 1975 and directed the CNO Strategic Studies Group from 1989 to 1992. He served as Assistant Secretary of the Navy (Installations and Environment) from March 1994 to October 2000, Under Secretary of the Navy from 12 October 2000 to 20 January 2001, and acting Secretary of the Navy January to May 2001.
102. Vice Admiral Robert Burns Pirie (1905–1990) was a 1926 graduate of the U.S. Naval Academy. He served in World War II in the Atlantic and on his retirement in 1962 was Deputy Chief of Naval Operations.

very famous naval officer. And later during my time as CNO, it was retired admiral Jim Hogg[103] who ran the SSG.

Anyway, this group, in simplest terms, tried to help the CNO deal with issues, and over the years it had varied between issues today that I'm dealing with or project me out twenty years or ten years or whatever it may be. So you'd spend a year together researching and thinking and gaming and trying to develop a product that you give back to the CNO that would help him deal with whatever the issue of the day was, and they do that to this day. So it was a very good experience, plus I got to deal with really good guys and folks that I hadn't dealt with before, SWO,[104] submarine.

JR: Non-aviators.

JJ: Yeah, exactly. I'd done that before, at Sixth Fleet and other places, but it was a great experience.

JR: What issues were you working on in SSG?

JJ: Most of what was being done at that time had to do with the future and warfare applications for the future, and this was Admiral—I want to say it was Carl Trost[105] who

---

103. Admiral (ret) James Robert Hogg (b. 1934) is a 1956 graduate of the U.S. Naval Academy. He commanded the U.S. Seventh Fleet 1983–1985. Hogg retired in 1991. In July 1995 he was appointed the director of the Chief of Naval Operations Strategic Studies Group and served in that role until 2013.
104. Surface Warfare Officer.
105. Admiral (ret) Carlisle Albert Herman Trost (b. 1930) served as the 23rd Chief of Naval Operations (CNO) and a member of the Joint Chiefs of Staff from 1986 to 1990. He is a 1953 graduate of the U.S. Naval Academy.

was the CNO when I was at the SSG. I can find perhaps what our work represented for you. I think I've got it somewhere. I'll try to dig that up.

JR: That'd be great.

JJ: But it was a good year, and that's the way it's designed. It's a one-year shot, then you're off. Then they bring in another group for the next year and so it goes. As I said, it's still going.

JR: Just to fill in some blanks, did you do senior-level school?

JJ: That was more or less my senior-level-equivalent school, and that's as close as I got to it. I'd gone to the Armed Forces Staff College[106]—we didn't talk about that—when I was a lieutenant commander in '76, but at that time that was a six-month deal. I did that on my way out of BuPers the first time en route to Miramar to learn how to fly the Tomcat.

JR: Any impressions of AFSC?

JJ: Yeah. One lasting impression is, as I recall, the guy who was the commandant was Rear Admiral Jeremiah Denton.[107]

---

106. The Armed Forces Staff College was established in 1946 to provide joint, operational level warfighting education. It was renamed the Joint Forces Staff College in 2000 and is located in Norfolk, Virginia.

107. Senator and Rear Admiral (ret) Jeremiah Andrew Denton Jr. (1924–2014) was a member of the class of 1947 at the U.S. Naval Academy. He was widely known for enduring eight years of imprisonment in North Vietnam from 1965 to 1973 and was the author of the best-selling memoir *When Hell Was In Session*. He represented Alabama in the U.S. Senate 1981–1987.

JR: No kidding.

JJ: So that makes an impression.

JR: No doubt.

JJ: Yeah. But I guess it's still going in some form. I don't even know if they call it Armed Forces Staff College anymore.

JR: No, it transitioned to JFSC in—

JJ: That's right. Joint Forces Staff College.

JR: I don't know if that got the axe when Joint Forces Command shut down or not. I'd have to check. I know that JSFC—I don't know. You didn't have to deal with JPME.[108]

JJ: Oh, yeah.

JR: Different requirements. But there's something about JPME Two, that Joint Forces Staff College was the only provider of this particular check for that block.

JJ: JPME Two?

---

108. Joint Professional Military Education.

JR: JPME Phase Two, which was like an additional jointness thing. In fact, that was the whole rationale for Joint Forces Staff College to exist, so far as I knew, is it provided that. No one else could provide that.

JJ: Interesting.

JR: Whether that has changed, I don't know, because my information is probably ten years out of date at this point.

JJ: Mine's worse than that. But that was the original context, I think, for the Armed Forces Staff College. It was sort of before jointness but not really, but that was, in many cases, the first exposure to all the other services, and I think in its time it was very good and helpful to give you a sense of perspective and appreciation for what the other guys are doing, as well as them hearing what goes on in this Navy.

JR: So when you were there at AFSC, there were multi-service—

JJ: Yeah.

JR: International? Were there foreign guys there?

JJ: I believe the answer is yes. Now, I'm hesitating because I'm trying to pull a name out and I don't have one handy, but I think the answer was yes. But most of my memory is of Army and Marine and Air Force guys at that time who were there. It was just a different perspective on our military lives, which is really kind of neat.

JR: So it was valuable?

JJ: Oh, yeah, indeed. And I always wish I had gotten a chance, to be honest with you, to go to National or Naval War College other than SSG, but it just didn't work out, or Monterey, for that matter.

JR: It doesn't seem to have hurt your career. [*Laughs*]

JJ: Yeah, but if there were a do-over, I'd do some of that stuff. You know how that goes.

JR: Sure. So, actually, there are two themes that we can take from this that will develop in future interviews. One would be strategic-level thinking in future warfare concepts from the sea and looking ahead, and then the other is jointness and how that all starts to play out, because in the nineties and when you were CNO, these are critical issues that people are trying to grapple with.

JJ: Yeah.

JR: So it's more than we can do today, but thinking ahead, this is kind of the germ of that, the root of these two themes.

Let's see. Well, I guess we have to talk about Tailhook[109] and that whole thing. Of course, it was a big scandal at the time, and even as I was reading through your Senate confirmation hearing from June of '96, even then people were talking about it.

JJ: Oh, yeah. It was still a really big deal.

JR: Five years later, in a town where two weeks later is an eternity.

JJ: Yeah, yeah.

JR: And this thing just kept being mentioned. In fact, when I was teaching at Quantico[110] in the late nineties, you'd still hear people talking about it.

JJ: Yeah, yeah.

JR: So what was it that made that particular—because Tailhook, as an event, had been going on for a while.

JJ: Yeah, been going on for a long time.

---

109. At the 35th Annual Tailhook Association Symposium September 8–12, 1991, at the Las Vegas Hilton in Las Vegas, Nevada, more than one hundred U.S. Navy and U. S. Marine Corps aviation officers were alleged to have engaged in "improper and indecent" conduct.
110. Marine Corps Base Quantico, Virginia, home of Marine Corps University.

JR: Yeah. And, you know, aviators do things. You get guys who let their hair down, they do crazy stuff. But why was 1991 such a cause? Why did it become such a scandal?

JJ: I guess in general terms, my sense of it would be that—and this is looking back over the shoulder, obviously—we were moving into different times, I guess is a way to say, and it wasn't just a bunch of guys anymore, okay? And the force was more diverse, and in large measure we weren't in phase with that. You know, you can fault a lot of things and a lot of people, but the bottom line, to me, is we just got out of phase with the times. Whether it was ever right, people can have their own views on all of that, but I think to a certain extent, as I said, we were out of phase with the times and then it got politicized and the Navy lost control of it for lots of different reasons. And putting that back in the box, if you will, putting it back in bounds was a long-term effort. I'd never been to Tailhook in my life.

JR: Before then?

JJ: Before then. And honestly really never wanted to go, for no particular reason, just—and I got assigned to go because I was the head of distribution for the Navy as a one-star, so I got orders to go to Tailhook.

JR: Why?

JJ: Because I was on a panel, making a presentation to a group of flag officers on naval aviation. So I went and did my panel, went home, and all hell broke loose. [*Laughter*]

JR: Read about it in the paper?

JJ: Yeah.

JR: Because that's what Tailhook was supposed to be, was a professional—

JJ: Professional symposium, yeah. Indeed. And I believe it is today.

JR: Sure.

JJ: But in some instances got carried away and out of phase with the realities of the day, and naval aviation paid a horrible price for it, in my opinion.

JR: Well, because the way it was represented later, in some kind of hysterical reporting, because reporters don't always know, and made it seem as though the purpose of Tailhook was to have this misbehavior and kind of lost sight of what it was supposed to be—

JJ: Exactly.

JR: And then you had these guys after hours, not as part of the—

JJ: Professional symposium, yeah.

JR: Yeah. It wasn't part of the symposium. It was just guys doing stuff offline that kind of cast a pall on it.

JJ: Indeed. And I do remember when I became CNO it was still a big issue, not at least in my domain because I was wearing naval aviator wings and I'd been to Tailhook, and I know a lot of people and a lot of my friends felt that, "Okay, now we've got an aviator as the CNO. We're going to get this Tailhook out of here. We're done with it. Okay, we've paid our price. We're done."

And I remember probably thinking to myself at that time that, "You know what? Yeah, it's time to get this thing behind us and move forward, learn the lessons and move forward." And I was stunned at how Washington was absolutely catatonic about Tailhook. I wasn't prepared for that. And I had friends say, "Why don't you do this? Why don't you do that?" And I said, "Let me tell you something. What you just suggested to me is a very logical pathway. It won't work in this town. I'm telling you it's a life of its own that bears no semblance to rational thinking in some respects." So you had to chip away at it as best you could incrementally, to try to put it to bed, so to speak, and get it over with. But it cost some really good naval officers their careers, and I regret that. I couldn't save some of them. And in my opinion and I think most everybody else's, they deserved saving. They didn't do anything.

JR: They were in the wrong place at the wrong time.

JJ: Yeah. And people have very strong views about all of that, but naval aviation paid a hell of a price for the acts of a few, and that's regrettable.

JR: So it was a few troublemakers and then press sensationalizing stuff.

JJ: It didn't help. Anything fact-based kind of got lost in the firestorm. It's too bad.

JR: Yeah. Well, it's important to get this recorded for posterity that it wasn't what it was portrayed in some of the more hysterical press reports.

JJ: Yes. But I think, again from my perspective, the biggest regret I have is that there were good men whom I knew well whose careers were terminated because of that, and in some cases that was really unfair and I couldn't do a damn thing about it.

JR: Important to note. Your first point about the culture shift is important.

JJ: Yeah.

JR: But also that individuals paying prices they shouldn't pay for larger-scale issues is another important point.

JJ: Yeah. Anyway, it was a very troubling time.

JR: Do you think that the Navy generally, naval aviation, has recovered from that? Does it still elicit the same response?

JJ: Tailhook?

JR: Yeah.

JJ: I don't know, is probably the best answer, because I'm not that close to it anymore. I don't know. I don't know if it's ever talked about in that context of Tailhook '91. A lot of the naval aviators weren't around then.

JR: That's true. [*Laughter*] Twenty-four years ago, yeah.

JJ: It's ancient history to most of them, so I don't think—my sense would be I'd be surprised if it was still resonating somewhere there. Naval aviation, I think, has moved well beyond that.

JR: Or in Washington.

JJ: Yeah.

JR: So right after that I have you as commander of Carrier Group 8.[111]

JJ: Mm-hmm.

JR: *Theodore Roosevelt*[112] battle group?

JJ: I did. It was great. That was the time when Admiral Paul David Miller,[113] who was CinCLant[114] in those days, and Admiral Hank Mauz[115] was CinCLantFlt,[116] as I recall, when, among other things that were being dealt with, we formed what was called the Marine Special MAGTF,[117] Marine Air-Ground Task Force, and embarked it in *Theodore Roosevelt* and deployed it to the Med, one of PDM's new deployment—not a scheme. It was a new deployment protocol, so to speak, and so the workup in the deployment of that battle group with a Special MAGTF embarked was really interesting and a good thing at that time. We learned a lot.

JR: So you're testing the new capability—

---

111. Carrier Group 8 is currently Carrier Strike Group 8, stationed at Norfolk, Virginia.
112. USS *Theodore Roosevelt* (CVN 71) is a *Nimitz*-class aircraft carrier launched in 1984. It is named for the 26th president of the United States.
113. Admiral (ret) Paul David Miller (b. 1941) joined the Navy in 1964 and upon retirement in 1994 was commander in chief of the U.S. Atlantic Command.
114. Commander in chief United States Atlantic Command.
115. Admiral (ret) Henry H. Mauz Jr. (b. 1936) was commander in chief United States Atlantic Fleet from 1992 to 1994. He graduated from the United States Naval Academy in 1959 and during the Vietnam War served with riverine units operating in the Mekong Delta.
116. Commander in chief Atlantic Fleet.
117. Marine Air Ground Task Force.

JJ: New operational concept to embark the Marines on the carrier with the air wing. Everybody's there. So we did that. It was really something. And I can tell you one side effect, nontrivial, by the way, although it may sound otherwise, when we got the Marines aboard the carrier, as you would expect, Marines are pretty physically fit, out of necessity, and so the whole physical regimen onboard that carrier changed, and we had a lot of Navy personnel who—my words, and I don't think I'm overdramatizing it—changed their lives on that deployment and either quit smoking, lost a bunch of weight, *really* got seriously committed to being in shape because they watched these Marines and then started working with them. I mean, from a physical fitness standpoint, it was unbelievable what was happening aboard *TR*. It was good.

JR: No kidding.

JJ: Yeah. To the point where we tried to ban smoking from *Theodore Roosevelt,* and we were actually doing it. And I'll never forget Admiral Kelso called the commanding officer of the ship—I think we were deployed at the time—Stan Bryant,[118] who was a great CO, and had to tell him that we couldn't ban smoking. Guess why. Because the tobacco lobby got to Congress, who got to the CNO, said, "You can't do that."

JR: That's interesting. [*Laughs*]

---

118. Rear Admiral (ret) Stanley W. Bryant is a 1969 graduate of the U.S. Naval Academy. He flew A-6 missions during the Vietnam War and was awarded three Distinguished Flying Crosses. At the time of his retirement in 2006 he was deputy commander to U.S. Naval Forces in Europe.

JJ: Yeah. And the CNO was very apologetic and said, "[unclear], Stan. You have no idea how it hurts me to have to tell you this, but this is what I have to tell you."

JR: What was Admiral Kelso's role at that time?

JJ: He was the Chief of Naval Operations.

JR: Huh.

JJ: Yeah. I think, for the most part, nobody smoked anyway by that point. It was in the early days of that, "that" being "Let's try to improve our physical fitness, stop smoking or reduce the smoking a lot, and put programs in place that would help sailors do that," help sailors and Marines do that. But that was an interesting reality check for the fleet.

JR: How did that change over the years? I mean, the smoking, drinking—

JJ: In the smoking instance, back when I was on the *Oriskany*, that's when we had the old reel movies, you know, the big reels, and you'd watch the movies in the ready room, and every ready room chair had an ashtray in it, and a lot of the guys smoked, so you could hardly see the screen sometimes from the smoke. [*Laughter*] That's just the way it was then, shall we say. And that's all changed. Now—I say "now." I'm so out of date now, but even when I left, the ships had designated smoking areas and that was all. If you wanted to smoke, you had to go basically outside, usually on the weather deck or something, out on the sponson on a carrier to smoke. So I think it's changed a lot, for the better, over the years, and I'm sure—I'd be shocked if the physical fitness thing wasn't a big part of life at sea these days.

JR: That improved over the years that you were doing this.

JJ: Yeah.

JR: More emphasis on that.

JJ: We put physical fitness standards in place and everybody had to meet them every year. Frankly, part of that was why I decided, when I was CNO, that I was going to run marathons.

JR: To set that example that you wanted.

JJ: Yeah. So I ran the Marine Corps Marathon twice as the CNO.

JR: That's really good. Have subsequent CNOs been out there?

JJ: I don't know the answer to that. I'm not aware of any. I tried to bait Chuck Krulak,[119] the commandant of the Marine Corps, into running it with me, but he didn't take the bait.

[*Laughter*]

JR: Yeah, that could lead to who knows what. [*Laughter*]

Well, this is when we're getting up to JTF 120. I don't know if you want to get into that now or we could just stop and discuss the next time.

JJ: Yeah, why don't we save it. That's good. That's good.

[End of October 28, 2015 interview]

---

119. General (ret) Charles Chandler Krulak (b. 1942) served as the 31st commandant of the Marine Corps 1995–1999. He is a 1964 graduate of the U.S. Naval Academy. He served two tours of duty in Vietnam where he was awarded the Silver Star, among other commendations. He is the son of Lieutenant General Victor H. "Brute" Krulak, USMC (1913–2008), a member of the Naval Academy Class of 1934 who served in World War II, Korea, and Vietnam.

Interview Number 2 with Admiral Jay L. Johnson, USN (Ret.)

Date: 21 March 2016

James Robbins (JR): This is James Robbins. It is March—

Jay Johnson (JJ): Twenty-one.

JR: Twenty-one.

JJ: First full day of spring.

JR: First day of spring. Talking to Admiral Jay Johnson, former CNO, as part of the Naval Institute Oral History Project.

Let's see. Where we left off was about 1991–1992. So in October 1992, you reported as commander for Carrier Group 8, commander of USS *Theodore Roosevelt*[120] battle group.

JJ: Yes.

JR: What were the major operations? This is post–[Operation] Desert Storm, when we were doing air suppression and other things over Iraq.[121] What did the *Roosevelt* battle group do?

---

120. USS *Theodore Roosevelt* (CVN 71) is a *Nimitz*-class aircraft carrier launched in 1984. It is named for the 26th president of the United States.

JJ: Let's see. This was the one where Admiral Paul David Miller[122] was CinCLant at that time, as I recall, and we did the Special Marine Air-Ground Task Force deployment aboard the carrier.[123] I think that's right. Yeah, Special MAGTF,[124] which was a means of trying to employ/deploy a Marine group on a CVN, CV, CNV,[125] just to put more—my words—flexibility and more agility into an operational situation. It had a lot of followers and it had a lot of unfollowers. [*Laughs*] It was pretty emotional, in many respects, but I thought it was a very forward-thinking and forward-leaning idea and we did a good job with it.

JR: You were testing these new concepts.

JJ: New concepts, new operational concepts. That's exactly right.

JR: New equipment?

---

121. Operation Desert Storm, January 17 to February 28, 1991, was the code name for the thirty-five-nation coalition effort to expel Iraqi forces that had invaded and occupied Kuwait. After the conflict phase, the United States participated in the enforcement of no-fly zones in northern and southern Iraq (Operations Northern and Southern Watch, respectively) under the auspices of United Nations Security Council Resolution 688. The no-fly zone operations lasted until the coalition invasion of Iraq in March 2003.
122. Admiral (ret) Paul David Miller (b. 1941) joined the Navy in 1964 and upon retirement in 1994 was commander in chief of the U.S. Atlantic Command.
123. This deployment was March–September 1993.
124. Marine Air Ground Task Force. The Special Purpose MAGTF (SPMAGTF) is a unit organized to accomplish a specific mission, operation, or regionally focused exercise, including training exercises, crisis response, or contingency operations.
125. CVN = Nuclear aircraft carrier. CV = Aircraft carrier. CNV does not appear in the DOD Dictionary of Military and Associated Terms.

JJ: For the most part, as I recall, not new equipment, but we embarked an entire task force of Marines permanently—"permanently"—for the workup in the deployment, which I don't think had been done before, and took them to the Med.

JR: What were the detractors saying?

JJ: "Well, we already have a means of deploying Marines in our amphibious forces, so why would you need to do this in a carrier battle group?" basically. But it taught us a lot, I guess is the fairest way to say it, and I'm quite sure it hasn't been done again. At that time I thought it was a good chance to learn, and we did. In a way, this is small in the grand scheme of big Navy, big Marine Corps, but I thought it was a great opportunity to enrich the relationship between the two Navy Department services, and we got a lot out of it, both Navy and Marine Corps.

This is perhaps a nonoperational story, but it's so true and it was powerful at the time. We had to accommodate this Marine Task Force into the life of the carrier, which was a different dynamic, and most of the Navy deployers were conscious of their physical fitness. We'd run on the flight deck or work out and do things. When the Marines came aboard, it was up an order of magnitude or two. [*Laughs*] But the really neat part of that was—initially it was just the Marines, they were doing their physical regimen. Then it changed over time, and pretty soon it was all of us, and the physical fitness of that carrier, I dare say, was better than probably any other ship in the Navy by the time we got back, and there were people—"people." I remember officers, chief petty officers, enlisted men who—

[Begin File 2]

JJ: I remember officers, chief petty officers, enlisted men who quit smoking, lost twenty pounds, and were really proud of that. So an unplanned benefit of the integration of the MAGTF on the carrier was a pretty fit crowd. [*Laughter*]

JR: Wow. Well, there you go.

JJ: That's probably not what they expected to get out of it, but it happened. It was really neat.

JR: Unforeseen benefits.

JJ: Yeah.

JR: What were some of the operational lessons learned from that?

JJ: That it could be done, that they could be used, that they could be employed from an aircraft carrier, they could be protected. So I think it met the criteria that Admiral Miller and others had envisioned on the front end, but as I say, while I'm not sure it's happened since then, we do have it in the kit bag if we ever need it again. Beyond that, I'm not sure. We could dig out the after-action reports of the Special MAGTF. But I had great respect for Colonel John Schmitt and the team that he brought aboard, and we worked very closely together and learned a lot.

JR: He was the commander of the Special MAGTF?

JJ: Mm-hmm. Great guy.

JR: So, to your knowledge, that wasn't used in any of our subsequent operations?

JJ: Not that I'm aware of. It may have been, and my focus got shifted.

JR: So I have July 1994, you took command of U.S. Second Fleet,[126] Commander Striking Fleet Atlantic,[127] Joint Task Force 120[128] for the deployment to Haiti.[129]

JJ: Indeed, yeah. That Second Fleet, that was a great command. I loved my time at Second Fleet, and the Haiti operation was an incredible experience. Flagship was *Mount*

---

126. The Second Fleet was the United States Navy's operational fleet in the Atlantic with an area of responsibility from the North Pole to the Caribbean, and from the East Coast of the United States to the middle of the Atlantic. It was headquartered at Naval Station Norfolk. The Second Fleet was disestablished in September 2011 and its responsibilities transferred to United States Fleet Forces Command.
127. Striking Fleet Atlantic (SFL) was a NATO multinational combatant command within Second Fleet 1952–2005.
128. Joint Task Force 120 (JTF-120) was the designation for Second Fleet in the role of commanding joint operations in its area of responsibility. In this case JTF-120 was organized for Operation Uphold Democracy, the U.S.-led intervention in Haiti, September 19, 1994, to March 31, 1995.
129. Operation Uphold Democracy was a U.S.-led intervention in Haiti, September 19, 1994, to March 31, 1995. It removed the regime of General Joseph Raoul Cédras, who had overthrown the elected government of President Jean-Bertrand Aristide in 1991. The operation was authorized by United Nations Security Council Resolution 940 on July 31, 1994.

Whitney.[130] That was the Second Fleet flagship, and we embarked the joint task force in *Mount Whitney* and went to Haiti with General Hugh Shelton[131] as the commander and me as the deputy commander of the joint task force, and spent a good bit of time down there.

We had the aircraft carrier *America*[132] down there with the Army Special Ops Aviation Group[133] embarked in *America,* so a variation on what we talked about before with the Special MAGTF, we did it this time with the joint task force Army-centric. It was [unclear], as I recall. But anyway, Doug Brown[134] and his team came aboard *America,* and they were some ways out from Port-au-Prince Harbor,[135] where we were. We didn't spend a lot of time there. Hugh and I were usually in a helicopter going somewhere in Haiti during that operation.

---

130. USS *Mount Whitney* (LCC/JCC 20) is a *Blue Ridge*–class command ship. From 1981 to 2005 it served as flagship for Commander Second Fleet/Commander Striking Fleet Atlantic. The ship is named for a peak in the Sierra Nevada mountains of California.
131. General Henry Hugh Shelton, U.S. Army (ret) (b. January 2, 1942) was the commander of the Army XVIII Airborne Corps and commanded the invasion force in Operation Uphold Democracy. General Shelton was commissioned through the ROTC program and served two tours of duty in Vietnam with the 5th Special Forces Group and 173rd Airborne Brigade. He commanded the 82nd Airborne Division and served as commander in chief of United States Special Operations Command (SOCOM). He later served as chairman of the Joint Chiefs of Staff, 1997–2001.
132. USS *America* (CVA/CV 66) was a *Kitty Hawk*–class supercarrier commissioned in 1965 and decommissioned in 1996. In 2005 *America* was scuttled southeast of Cape Hatteras.
133. The Army 160th Special Operations Aviation Regiment (SOAR) pioneered the "Adaptive Joint Force Package" concept during Operation Uphold Democracy by launching missions from the USS *America*.
134. General Doug Brown, U.S. Army (ret) (b. 1948) commanded the 160th Special Operations Aviation Regiment (SOAR) as a colonel during Operation Uphold Democracy. Brown enlisted in the Army in 1967 as a private and fought in Vietnam as part of a Special Forces "A" team. After his commissioning in May 1970, he returned to combat duty in Vietnam as a UH-1 helicopter pilot. He was one of the founding members of the 160th Special Operations Aviation Regiment in 1981. He later served as commander of Joint Special Operations Command (JSOC) 1998–2000, U.S. Army Special Operations Command (USASOC) 2000–2002, and U.S. Special Operations Command (USSOCOM) 2003–2007.
135. Port-au-Prince Harbor is the location of the seaport of the capital of Haiti, Port-au-Prince.

As you probably recall, we went down there with the intent and the direction to basically bring XVIII Airborne Corps[136] in and secure Haiti, and that got redirected as they were airborne. We spent a good bit of time there trying to stabilize and enable a change of leadership and help Haiti put itself right, which has been something we've been trying to do since the Marines were there in, what, the thirties. We covered every inch of Haiti many times and got to work with some really special people, like Police Commissioner Ray Kelly,[137] former Marine, always a Marine, who was brought down there on the police side of things, so we worked a lot with Ray. He had a daunting task to integrate the police efforts and basically grow a robust and incredible police force across the island of Haiti. It was quite an operation.

One of my most distinct memories of that was that the more we dealt with the Haitian people, I kept coming away and saying these are really good people. They just need some leadership. They need a chance. They're hardworking, they've been abused by their government, and they just need a chance. And that's probably the dominant thought I have from my time in Haiti, was I felt so sorry for the people of Haiti because it was hard to get a chance to succeed, but they were hardworking, they were good people in a really tough spot. The countryside had been denuded, the trees were gone in a lot of the areas because they needed it to stoke their little fires. I don't know. It's a beautiful place. It had been made not beautiful by circumstance. It's interesting.

---

136. The Army XVIII Airborne Corps is designated as a strategic response force, with its mission to "deploy on short-notice anywhere in the world by air, land, or sea to conduct unified land operations as an Army, Joint, or Combined Task Force Headquarters."
137. Raymond Walter Kelly (b. September 4, 1941) was the director of police under the United Nations mission in Haiti. He served as New York City police commissioner 1992–1994 and 2002–2013. He joined the U.S. Marine Corps in 1963 and was deployed to combat duty in Vietnam 1965–1966 as a lieutenant with 2nd Battalion 1st Marines. At the time of Operation Uphold Democracy, he was a colonel in the Marine Corps Reserves.

JR: Yeah, if you look at a satellite photo of the Dominican Republic[138]—

JJ: I was going to say, I've been to that border and there's no question where the border is. Where the trees start, that's the Dom Rep. [*Laughs*]

JR: Yes. It's different when you look at those photos.

JJ: Yeah, it really is. Anyway, so we did the Haitian operation in *Mount Whitney*.

JR: As you mentioned, it was supposed to be an invasion. You had planned for an invasion.

JJ: Indeed.

JR: What was the assessment if it had gone that way? I think our forces would have been able to handle whatever Haiti had.

JJ: Without question, yeah.

JR: High confidence.

JJ: Yes, there was indeed, but as you recall, there was an [inaudible] that night and the president made the call, and we waived off the invasion.

---
138. The Dominican Republic is east of Haiti and occupies two-thirds of the island of Hispaniola.

JR: Right. And they were literally in the air when General Cedras[139] stepped down.

JJ: They were in the air. That is correct. It's also where I really got to know and develop respect for and friendship, almost love, for Hugh Shelton. Amazing guy, General Shelton, fearless. He dealt with Cedras directly, and it was a thing of beauty to watch him.
[*Laughs*]

JR: How so? Can you expand on that a little?

JJ: Not really. Just you don't want Hugh Shelton in your face. [*Laughter*] He's a big man.

JR: I've seen him. He's a big guy.

JJ: Very imposing, but the words that come out of his mouth and the power behind them are very real, and that made an indelible impression on Mr. Cedras.

JR: All for the good, as it turned out.

---

139. Joseph Raoul Cédras (b. July 9, 1949) was a lieutenant general in the *Forces Armées d'Haïti* who organized a coup d'état against President Jean-Bertrand Aristide on September 29, 1991. He was de facto ruler of Haiti until being pressured to relinquish power on October 10, 1994, in the face of imminent invasion during Operation Uphold Democracy.

JJ: Yes, indeed. But it's interesting that since then, a lot has happened in Haiti, some good, a lot bad, but Presidents Clinton[140] and Bush 43[141] and others, I think that experience really put Haiti in the forefront of Mr. Clinton's thinking. I certainly can't speak for him, but if you just look at his follow-through with Haiti since that operation, it's very real and very sincere, in my opinion.

JR: How long was the joint task force down there?

JJ: I knew you were going to ask me that. I'd have to check the record, to be honest with you. It was, I want to say, a couple of months.

JR: But when the invasion was called off—

JJ: We stayed.

JR: And you switched into the other aspects of the operation.

JJ: Indeed, yeah.

JR: That was probably the Phase Four type of stuff that was already planned.

---

140. William Jefferson Clinton, the 42nd president of the United States, 1993–2001.
141. George Walker Bush, the 43rd president of the United States, 2001–2009.

JJ: Yeah, and so we stayed and we worked very hard to try to stabilize things, and for the most part at that time, I thought we accomplished that, but it's a long way up for them. If you ever want to see poverty, go to Cité Soleil[142] and just walk around, it's shocking. And again it gets back to my impression—those people just need a chance.

JR: From a jointness[143] point of view, looking at the operation, I read that someone said the counterexample was Grenada,[144] that there were lessons learned from Grenada that were to be applied to this operation. Did [Operation] Urgent Fury[145] inform you in any way in the planning?

JJ: I'm sure it probably did, but I couldn't give you a specific lesson learned that we—I just don't recall, to be honest.

JR: So it didn't stand out that much.

JJ: No.

---

142. Cité Soleil is an impoverished shanty town in the Port-au-Prince metropolitan area.
143. Jointness in this sense refers to cross-service cooperation particularly with respect to the system created by the Goldwater-Nichols Department of Defense Reorganization Act of October 4, 1986. The act was intended to address issues of inter-service rivalry, promote improved command and control in joint warfighting, and more rational and integrated procurement practices. It was in part a response to problems that had arisen with joint coordination during Operation Urgent Fury in 1983 (see below), during which American forces were killed in inter-service friendly fire incidents.
144. A Caribbean island invaded during Operation Urgent Fury (see below).
145. Operation Urgent Fury (October 25–December 15, 1983) was a U.S.-led invasion of the Caribbean island of Grenada, undertaken to overthrow the communist government of Maurice Bishop and his New Jewel Movement and to secure the safety of six hundred U.S. medical students on the island.

JR: What were some of the lessons learned from this operation? I'm talking about jointness.

JJ: Well, I think that probably the biggest was that if you're willing to use your assets, tailor your assets to the task at hand and not get hung up on the way it's been, it's kind of a follow-through on the Special Marine Air-Ground Task Force. "What do you mean, you're going to fly the aircraft off the aircraft carrier and send it down there? You can't do that. We never do that." Turns out we did. So we had our fighters on the carrier as they came through, and then my recollection is we flew them on and put the Army in there or struck them below and put the Army on top. But the point is, tailoring the asset mix to do the task at hand, that's elemental jointness, and it really does work.

We did the Army Special Ops—I'm struggling for the name. I want to say Task Force 160.[146] Anyway, Doug Brown, Colonel Brown, now General Brown, retired. We did his change of command on the flight deck of USS *America,* which was pretty neat, in Haiti. The Army Special Ops Aviation Command change was right there on the carrier.

JR: Wow. That was probably a first.

JJ: Yeah, and we heloed over there from Port-au-Prince Harbor and then drove Special Ops fastboats back. I got to drive a Special Ops boat. That high-speed one-hour run back to Port-au-Prince Harbor, back to *Mount Whitney,* was great.

JR: For a Navy aviator, I bet that was a first too. [*Laughs*]

---
146. The Army 160th Special Operations Aviation Regiment (SOAR) (see above).

JJ: I don't know, but it was fun. It was a great trip, a good experience.

So, back to the question. It's the willingness of the leadership to accept the reality they're going into and tailor the force. We've got tremendous assets, equipment, troops, Special Ops, all manner, but to me, the strength of jointness is being willing to take that asset mix and put it in a way that makes sense for that situation, which is exactly what happened down there, and it worked.

JR: Did you run into any interoperability challenges?

JJ: I'm sure we did, but I'm also pretty sure we worked through them. I don't recall anything that, "Oh, we just broke the pencil." I don't remember any of that.

JR: Nothing had to be canceled or scratched?

JJ: Not that I recall at all, no.

JR: What's your view, in general, on jointness and the drive for a joint force and how far it can go?

JJ: Notwithstanding what I just said, I believe jointness is necessary. I believe that in some respects we've carried it too far, and by that I mean I think that the drive to make sure everyone's been joint-qualified as they proceed in seniority up the ranks in some respects has caused us to take our eye off our service-specific leadership roles. It becomes all-consuming in some ways. That overdramatizes it a little, but my point is, I think we have to be careful that our desire and need and legal requirement to get you or me into joint jobs as we go, sometimes that happens at the expense of service requirements and leadership roles. And I think we can get carried away with jointness, not with execution necessarily, but in the construct of what it takes to be joint. Don't forget, for Navy leadership, our primary task is to lead the United States Navy, and sometimes I worry that jointness dilutes that elemental requirement.

JR: The bureaucratized aspects of it, I guess.

JJ: Precisely.

JR: Always having to check certain blocks.

JJ: Yeah.

JR: Altering their career path in order to do that.

JJ: Yes. And I don't know, maybe it's fine now, but that would be my caution with jointness. Let's not get too carried away here.

JR: So you wouldn't be behind, for example, a joint service academy.

JJ: I definitely would not, no. Again, we have a great Navy, we have a great Army, we have a great Air Force, Coast Guard, Marine Corps, okay? I don't see the need strategically, operationally, tactically, morally, you pick the word—

JR: Culturally?

JJ: Culturally. I don't see it. I think one of our great strengths within the services is our ethos within that service, and we don't need to dilute the gene pool.

JR: So the Navy's traditions, its history—

JJ: Absolutely, absolutely.

JR: All of the things can be lost if you go too "purple."[147]

JJ: Yes. I really believe that, yeah.

JR: Yeah, I agree completely.

JJ: Yeah. There's no place for it. From any of the things I just mentioned, you know, from strategic all the way down to cultural, it serves no constructive purpose, in my view.

---

147. Purple in this context is reference to the color used to designate joint commands and billets.

JR: So jointness as an operational construct can make a lot of sense, as was your experience.

JJ: Yes.

JR: In other respects, don't go crazy on it.

JJ: That's exactly right.

JR: Yeah, I think that's about right.

JJ: Yeah. I'm long out of it now, but I think we need to be very alert to what brought us where we are as a service. And I say that from Navy, but it would be the same if I were an Army general retired or Marine or Coast Guard or any of them. Let's not lose the service leadership, integrity, and requirement and really purpose. Let's not dilute that in the name of jointness.

JR: So would you say that there's a synergy from the differences from the services?

JJ: I do.

JR: When they come together in a joint environment, they bring different things together, and create something.

JJ: Yes. And again, as long as you're willing to accept the uniqueness of each of them and blend them together in a way that makes sense for whatever it is you're trying to accomplish, taking most of the aircraft off an aircraft carrier as it deploys into an area like the Haitian operation, it works. You've got to be willing to make those leadership decisions.

JR: What do you think the drive is for this ultra jointness, you know, some really radical propositions about having people sort of skip between services, like SES is supposed to do, things like that?

JJ: I think it's another one of these theoretical ideas that are being generated by people who have no operational experience, just not great. The military services should not be an experiment. There's too much at stake. Grow and build within the individual services' historical strengths and tailor those strengths to today's reality and be proud of that, and let's not try to make it all a one-size-fits-all, because we'll lose.

JR: I've always thought there was something to be said for the morale aspects of the service rivalries. It's not always a negative to have service rivalries.

JJ: Good lord, no, not at all. [*Laughs*] No. It's very healthy and, I think, very necessary, and it's okay. At the end of the day, you and I may be service rivals, you Air Force and me Navy, but at the end of the day, we're probably going to go out and have a beer together.

JR: All right. Trade stories.

JJ: Yeah.

JR: Your previous example of the beneficial effect of having Marines on a carrier.

JJ: Yes, exactly.

JR: That inspired the sailors in ways they wouldn't admit, but— [*Laughs*]

JJ: Yes.

JR: You took over as acting CNO in May 1996, when Mike Boorda[148] shot himself.

JJ: Yes.

JR: Any impressions on that? I mean, that's a very controversial incident.

---

148. Admiral Jeremy Michael Boorda (November 26, 1939–May 16, 1996) served as the 25th Chief of Naval Operations, 1994–1996. He joined the Navy as an enlisted sailor in 1956 and was commissioned as an ensign after completing Officer Candidate School in 1962. He served a combat tour in Vietnam in 1965 and afterward held several surface warfare commands. Other important assignments included chief of naval personnel/deputy chief of naval operations for manpower, personnel and training; commander in chief, Allied Forces Southern Europe; and commander in chief, U.S. Naval Forces, Europe. He was noted for being the first enlisted sailor to rise through the ranks to become CNO.

JJ: [*sighs*] Well, it was a bad day, and I spent the whole morning with him. I was the vice chief. I'd been there, I guess, since February, and I thought the world of Mike Boorda. He was a great boss. He and "Skip" Bowman[149] and I—Skip was chief of naval personnel—spent that morning of the 16th of May doing basically flag detailing, which we did not infrequently.

People always ask me, "Well, did you see anything? Did you sense anything?" Of course the answer is no.

I had to go to lunch with John Douglass,[150] who was the assistant secretary of the navy, one of the assistant secretaries, and we'd scheduled previously this lunch in the Pentagon, and I was late. I remember telling him, "I've got to go, boss. John Douglass is waiting for me."

He said, "You really have to go?"

I said, "Yeah, I do."

So I broke company and had my lunch, went back to my office. An hour later, the EA came in and told me what had happened, and I couldn't believe it. So it was a bad day.

JR: Any insights as to why he would do that?

---

149. Admiral Frank Lee "Skip" Bowman, U.S. Navy (ret.) (b. December 19, 1944) was chief of naval personnel 1994–1996. He later served as director of naval nuclear propulsion, from 1996 to his retirement in 2004.
150. Brigadier General John W. Douglass, USAF (ret.) (b. May 2, 1941) served as United States assistant secretary of the navy (Research, Development and Acquisitions) 1995–1998.

JJ: No. Is there really any insight to what straw breaks the camel's back in any suicide? I'm not put to say. And there are lots of stories and lots of opinions, but mine is here's a guy who just reached a breaking point and ended his life tragically. I was very sad for that. I felt very sorry for Mike and his family. Still do.

But he was the sailor's sailor, and the Navy loved him for that, which is different, as you know, and that's part of the history, non–Naval Academy, a former enlisted man who's now the CNO. That resonated powerfully with the sailors in the fleet, especially when they saw him and talked to him and interacted with him, because he was magical. He really was. It was unbelievable.

JR: And you had a good working relationship, I gather.

JJ: Sure. He was powerful on the [Capitol] Hill. He was just an amazing guy, but for probably lots of reasons, some may be obvious and many that probably aren't, it just got too much for him and he took his life.

JR: That's tragic.

JJ: Yeah. So by law, I became the acting CNO that day, and then went through the funeral and all of that. But I will say that that experience, one of the people that was really helpful to me through that was President Clinton, because he thought the world of Mike Boorda. I remember he came to the Pentagon and we were together alone, and he just put his arm around me and he said, "Hey, we're going to get through this, Jay, and I'll help you."

JR: No kidding. So the president personally was involved in this.

JJ: Yeah, yeah, he sure was.

So the few months between that and when—well, it wasn't really long. This was May 16, and I was acting, and within the next two, three weeks, the Navy Department and the DOD came to their decision on who they were going to nominate to be the next CNO. I remember being informed and then going to the White House on my fiftieth birthday, June 5, 1996, to sit down with the president in the Oval Office, and the secretary of defense[151] and the Joint Chiefs and others, to determine if I was going to pass muster with him on being the nominee. Amazing.

One of the things that I was trying to understand and cope with was how to get the Navy back on its feet, because it was a real blow to the United States Navy to have their CNO commit suicide, and I was getting that from everywhere, and especially the "sailor's sailor," if you know what I'm saying. I was just trying to come up with, okay, how do I articulate where I think we need to go to get our sailors and our Navy back on its feet again, if you will.

I ran a lot at that time, and my standard procedure during the day, if I was in Washington, was I'd get up at 4:30 or 5:00, put on my running gear. I lived at Foggy

---

151. At the time the secretary of defense was William J. Perry.

Bottom,[152] 2300 E Street. Run down to the Lincoln Memorial and then do laps in the dark or whenever it was, up to the Washington Monument and back, just me, and that's how I set my head for the day.

In the course of doing that after Mike died, as I knew I was being nominated, I developed the concept that I thought I needed to take to the Navy, and that's where "Steer by the Stars"[153] came from—the idea that it's time to quit hanging our heads. Let's pick ourselves up and move forward. It's a wonderful Navy. We've had a very tragic event, but it's time to move forward. So I developed the concept—I don't know if "concept" is the right word—called "Steer by the Stars," and the only way you can see the stars is if your head is held high. I said, "For us in the Navy, there are going to be four guide stars out there that are going to steer us, and those guide stars will be operational primacy, leadership, teamwork, and pride." And I developed from that shell the message I took to the Navy around the world as soon as I was confirmed.

I took that to the White House and told the president the idea, that we were going to steer by the stars ahead of us instead of the wake behind us, and the only way you can see those stars is by looking up, lift your head, and the key to all of it, I said, is going to be our great people. I've got a sheet here that encapsulates what I talked about.

But anyway, so on the 5th of June, as I recall, my fiftieth birthday, 1996, I was in the White House for my nomination as CNO.

JR: Wow.

---

152. Foggy Bottom is a neighborhood in the Northwest quadrant of Washington, D.C., from west of the White House to Rock Creek. The term is also a euphemism for the U.S. Department of State, which has its headquarters in that area.

153. "Steer by the Stars" was Adm. Johnson's vision statement for the U.S. Navy, emphasizing operational primacy, leadership, teamwork, and pride.

JJ: Yeah.

JR: How did that feel? It's kind of a career moment.

JJ: Yeah, it was definitely a career moment. [*Laughter*]

JR: Was that anything you'd ever envisioned?

JJ: No, of course not, no. Sometimes life comes at you in ways you didn't expect, and that was certainly one of them. It was not without its moments. I know, for example, that lots of senior admirals thought they'd be better positioned to be the CNO, and that may have been the case in some cases, but that wasn't what happened. For the most part, I got great support from the more senior admirals in the United States Navy who understood the situation. Admiral Bruce DeMars[154] stands out as somebody who's still a dear friend, he said, "Hey, I'll help you in any way I can." Somebody else who did that to me, for whom I still have the utmost respect, was General Colin Powell.[155] I didn't know him very well, but he made a point of telling me—he said, "I'm always here if you need me. I understand what you're going through. I'll never get in the way, but I'm always here if you need me." I thought that was pretty special.

---

154. Admiral Bruce DeMars, USN (ret.) (b. 1935) served as director, Naval Nuclear Propulsion, 1988–1996. He is a 1957 graduate of the United States Naval Academy.
155. Colin Luther Powell (b. April 5, 1937) is a retired U.S. Army general and served as 65th U.S. secretary of state 2001–2005. He served as national security advisor to President Ronald Reagan 1987–1989, and 12th chairman of the Joint Chiefs of Staff 1989–1993.

JR: Were there any other senior leaders at the time that you'd say were helping mentor you with your career or had helped get you to that position?

JJ: Well, Mike was certainly one of them, but I had a lot of help from—we talked about John Barrow and his influence on me. Another one is Admiral Jim Holloway,[156] former CNO. He was extremely helpful to me. Admiral Isaac Kidd[157] was extremely helpful to me as CNO, and one of the great privileges of my life was to deliver the eulogy at Admiral Kidd's funeral, because he was so important to me and such a marvelous human being. He would call and always just to talk, but he was doing a morale check, seeing if there was really anything he could do to help me, or just to listen, because he knew the complexities of what I was going through. So, some really special people helped me.

JR: So they gave you the benefit of their experience.

JJ: Absolutely. Admiral Chuck McGrail.[158] Lots of them.

But once I got confirmed, as I mentioned earlier, I then went on this kind of round-the-world tour, but what I was really doing was talking to the Navy and trying to

---

156. Admiral James Lemuel Holloway III, U.S. Navy (ret) (b. February 23, 1922) served as Chief of Naval Operations from 1974 to 1978. Holloway is a highly decorated aviator who served in World War II, the Korean War, and the Vietnam War. After Vietnam he was instrumental in developing the USS *Nimitz* and other supercarriers of its class. He is a June 1942 graduate of the U.S. Naval Academy and son of Admiral James Lemuel Holloway Jr. (1898–1984).
157. Admiral Isaac Campbell Kidd Jr. (August 14, 1919–June 27, 1999) served as commander in chief of the U.S. Atlantic Fleet from 1975 to 1978. He was a 1941 graduate of the U.S. Naval Academy and received his commission as an ensign on December 19, 1941, twelve days after his father, Rear Admiral Isaac C. Kidd, was killed on the bridge of his flagship, the battleship *Arizona,* during the Japanese attack on Pearl Harbor.
158. Admiral Charles Reynolds McGrail Jr. (November 24, 1935–December 21, 1998) was a 1957 graduate of the U.S. Naval Academy. He flew fighter missions in the Vietnam War and also was involved in planning air operations at Military Assistance Command, Vietnam (MACV). He later served in various command positions and on his retirement in 1991 was serving as assistant deputy chief of naval operations for naval warfare.

lift us back up and get this tragedy behind us, if you can ever really do that, and get on with it in a very positive way, because we had the best Navy in the world. We still do. So that's where "Steer by the Stars" became the message I carried. I could talk for two hours about it or I could talk for 45 seconds about it and everything in between, depending on where I was. I could tailor it to if I was talking to the chief's mess or if I was talking to the flag leadership. It was a great thought template for me and a very appropriate message for the Navy, and I think most folks got it. It resonated with them. The leadership of the Navy was very helpful to me, officer and enlisted leadership, in understanding that and then broadcasting it in their own way throughout the Navy so that we could, again, hold our heads high, because we had every right to.

JR: Who were you working with then when you took over in 1996 as CNO? In your immediate area, who did you report to?

JJ: Well, I reported to the CNO as the vice chief, but I also worked with guys like General Joe Ralston,[159] Air Force, and lots of others. There's another officer that you asked me about who was really helpful to me and who kind of mentored me. The other name that really sticks out is Admiral Stan Arthur.[160] Stan has been helpful to me for most of my naval career and sets an amazing example in how to be a really good naval

---

159. General Joseph W. Ralston, USAF (ret.) (b. November 4, 1943) served as the vice chairman of the Joint Chiefs of Staff from 1996 to 2000.
160. Admiral Stanley R. Arthur, U.S. Navy (ret.) (b. September 27, 1935) served as vice chief of naval operations 1992–1995. He was a highly decorated combat aviator during the Vietnam War and held a number of important command positions during his career, including command of the United States Seventh Fleet and U.S. Naval Forces Central Command (USNAVCENT) during Operation Desert Storm in 1991.

officer and also how to live your life. Stan Arthur is a remarkable man. So he was another one.

I had an interesting experience not long ago again. And I told you about Admiral Jim Holloway, who's now in his nineties, amazing man, class of 1943 Naval Academy. One of his dear friends and compatriots in a way, a fellow aviator, is George Herbert Walker Bush.[161] I tell both of them—and I got to do it again only about three weeks ago—that "in terms of influences on this naval aviator's life, you two set the standard for me." I consider their mentorship and friendship to be among the greatest gifts I've ever had, and I tell them both that. Remarkable.

JR: I think it's an important thing for junior officers, folks coming up, to understand is that you don't get to where you get all on your own.

JJ: No. And to this day I'll still have people say, "Well, now, how do you set yourself up to become the CNO?"

I say, "You don't."

"Well, were you always going to be a career naval officer?"

"No."

"When you graduated from the Naval Academy, did you want to be an admiral?"

"No. I wanted to be a fighter pilot. And guess what? I was." And I said my view was always as long as I feel like I'm making a contribution and that I'm challenged and

---

161. George Herbert Walker Bush was the 41st president of the United States, 1989–1993. He was an aviator in the U.S. Navy 1942–1945 serving in the Pacific Theater and was awarded the Distinguished Flying Cross.

that I like what I'm doing and trying to make a difference for the Navy, I'm going to stay in. And one thing leads to another, and thirty-two-and-some years later, I'm still there.

I told the midshipmen at the Naval Academy, when I was CNO I gave one of the Forrestal Lectures,[162] and I said, "Look. I know what you're thinking. 'When is this old fart going to be done? I've got stuff to do.'" I said, "Because I've been there, okay? That's exactly what I thought lo those many years ago. But here's what I'm going to tell you, the most important thing I'm going to tell you tonight, and this isn't in my script. You have no idea, you have no idea right now how fast your life is going to pass you. I remember distinctly sitting where you are," and at that time it was 30-some years ago. And I said, "It goes by in the blink of an eye. You don't believe that now, but when you get to be my age, and I don't consider myself an old guy, you do, but I don't. I'm 53 years old," or whatever I was then, somewhere between 50 and 54. I said, "It's the blink of an eye. That's how fast it goes when you're looking at it from my side. What's the moral to that story? Why am I telling you that? I'm telling you that because don't ever, don't waste a minute of it, okay? Don't waste a minute of it, because you have no idea how fast it goes by."

Anyway, I hadn't really thought about saying that until I just started looking into their faces, and it just carried me right back to where they were. [*Laughs*]

JR: So when you took over in June of '96, you mentioned "Steer by the Stars" and raising the morale of the force, but what were some of the challenges that you faced as CNO?

---

162. The Forrestal Lecture Series was established at the U.S. Naval Academy in May 1970 in honor of the late secretary of defense James V. Forrestal (1892–1949) who, as Secretary of the Navy, was instrumental in the development of the modern Navy.

JJ: Well, the biggest challenge I had, frankly, was getting the Navy adjusted to a new leader, and that wasn't a two-month experience; that took a while. I don't mean that negatively. It just took a while because for all the strengths of Mike Boorda, he did things in some respects differently. I didn't have the reach that he had. I didn't have the connections with Congress and the legislators that he did. He was universally revered and respected, and I'm the new guy, so I had a lot of work to do to bring myself into that, not at his level, I never got to his level, but to build relationships that were important to the Navy. So that was the biggest challenge I had, for at least the first year or two.

I got great support from the Hill. They understood that I wasn't Mike Boorda. But working with the leadership over there, I revered Ted Stevens,[163] Senator Stevens, Senator Inouye,[164] John McCain,[165] and others were very helpful to me and very supportive of our Navy and understanding. So that was the biggest challenge for me.

Also, back to Mike, if Seaman Jones had an issue, he would talk to the CNO about it directly if he saw him or sent him an email or whatever, and so the chain of command in some respects felt like, "Hey, what about me? I'll take care of Seaman Jones. He works for me." I don't want to overplay that, but that was an issue for some of the leadership within the Navy, so it was important to me that the Navy reinvigorate or

---

163. Senator Theodore Fulton "Ted" Stevens Sr. (November 18, 1923–August 9, 2010) was a United States senator from Alaska 1968–2009. He served in the Army Air Forces in the Second World War, flying transport aircraft in the China-Burma-India theater. He was a recipient of the Distinguished Flying Cross among other commendations.
164. Daniel Ken "Dan" Inouye (September 7, 1924–December 17, 2012) was a United States senator from Hawaii 1963 to 2012. He was a captain in the U.S. Army during the Second World War, serving with the 442nd Infantry Regiment. During the Italian campaign he lost his right arm to a grenade wound. He was the recipient of many awards including the Distinguished Service Cross, which was upgraded to the Medal of Honor by President Bill Clinton.
165. John Sidney McCain III (born August 29, 1936) is the senior United States senator from Arizona, first elected in 1987. He is a 1958 graduate of the U.S. Naval Academy and son of 1931 graduate John Sidney "Jack" McCain Jr. (January 17, 1911–March 22, 1981). He was wounded during the 1967 USS *Forrestal* fire (see first interview). McCain was shot down on October 26, 1967, during his twenty-third bombing mission over North Vietnam, and remained a POW for five and a half years until March 14, 1973. He retired from the Navy as a captain in 1981.

reinforce the chain of command without losing the openness and the caring that the direct approach of Admiral Boorda, that that direct approach was still felt throughout the fleet. You don't want to destroy that, but there are ways to do it and still use the chain of command.

It gets back to my "Steer by the Stars" and the articulation of that and the commitment of that down through the chain of command to make the leadership at all levels more engaging with the people they're working for and with so that you have that dialogue without necessarily saying, "I don't ever want you writing to the CNO." You don't need a directive that says that. If the leadership is really engaged, it takes care of itself. So getting that permeated throughout the Navy was another part of the challenge, really. Now, I'm not talking about ships and airplanes and budgets and all that. I had wonderful vice chiefs that helped me do a lot of that. But I was working very hard to get the Navy to reinforce the strength of the chain of command and the engagement of that chain of command at all levels in a very transparent manner. It's a long answer to your question.

JR: That's good. What was the role of the CNO at that time? What were your areas of responsibility?

JJ: Well, you're the organize, train, and equip, Title X[166] guy. By law, that's what you do. So, worked a lot with the fleet commanders, worked a lot the Secretariat, worked a lot with the Joint Staff, but again, the service chief's role was organize, train, and equip. I

---

166. Title X refers to Title 10 U.S. Code, which governs the armed forces. Subtitle C, the Navy and Marine Corps, details organization, personnel, education and training, and general administration of the naval forces, which were the primary concern of the CNO.

don't think that's changed. I think there's a lot of discussion right now on should Goldwater-Nichols[167] be revised. So they've got lots of people looking at that and lots of opinions flying around. I think it's probably appropriate to look at it, since it's been, what, 1980-something, was it?

JR: Eighty-six.

JJ: Eighty-six, yeah. So again, let's put the cards on the table and see what's working for us today and what isn't, and how can we do it better, and be bold enough to change.

JR: Oh, sure. I've always thought the implementation—my personal opinion—of Goldwater-Nichols has been a work in progress, anyway.

JJ: Mm-hmm.

JR: When you talk about changing it, it's been changing all the time.

JJ: Yeah, yeah.

JR: Because people draw different things out of it. The thing is so big that when you got down to actually doing something with it, my experience in government, watching different joint aspects of Goldwater-Nichols implementation, the thing has changed—it

---

167. The Goldwater-Nichols Department of Defense Reorganization Act of October 4, 1986 (see note above).

just depends on who's reading it. So when they say, "Let's revise it," go ahead. It's already been revised, but take your shot.

JJ: Yeah.

JR: That's my take on it.

JJ: But, for example, one of the things that I always felt, and I think subsequent service chiefs or CNOs have felt, is that we were taken out of the acquisition side of things in large measure by Goldwater-Nichols, and that went to the Secretariat. I always felt like at the end of the day, if something goes wrong with a program, I know who they're going to call, and it won't be the Secretariat; they're going to call the CNO. I've had a few of those calls. [*Laughs*] I said, "Hey, pal, I hear what you're saying, but I didn't have a thing to do with that decision, because I couldn't." So that's one of the things that I think constructively they're looking at to see if the uniformed service side of the acquisition business should be revised or adjusted. In my opinion, it should be. CNO ought to be engaged in that.

JR: Why do you suppose they're looking at that change? It's just gone too far?

JJ: Yeah. It's to your point. The thing has morphed itself in many respects, but that one, I think it must be changed. It can't just happen. I think they would have to adjust or modify or update, however you want to say it, that aspect of Goldwater-Nichols, to make it so.

JR: What were some of the major programs that you oversaw or at least happened on your watch?

JJ: Well, I'll talk to one, because it was really most important to the Navy at the time, and that was the F-18 Super Hornet,[168] which was in development and not without its controversies. "Why do we need this?" This was about the time that the Joint Strike Fighter[169] was birthing. The concept was becoming more of a reality. "Why would you need to spend all this money on this new Super Hornet for carrier fleets when you've got this Joint Strike Fighter that's going to be there before you know it?"

So it was a fight inside the Pentagon, and on Capitol Hill somewhat, but mostly inside the Pentagon, and we were at risk of losing that program, so we fought very hard inside the lifelines and outside the lifelines to garner support for the Super Hornet. One of the things I'm most proud of during my time as CNO is that we prevailed. Admiral John Lockard,[170] who was running NavAir[171] at the time, and I and others spent a lot of time with the secretary of defense, who at that time was Bill Cohen,[172] and to his credit, he supported it, as did the president. We have a bunch of F-18 E/F Super Hornets right now,

---

168. The Boeing F/A-18E and F/A-18F Super Hornet are twin-engine carrier-capable multirole fighter aircraft variants based on the McDonnell Douglas F/A-18 Hornet. The Super Hornet became operational in 1999 as a replacement for the F-14 Tomcat.
169. The Joint Strike Fighter (JSF) is a multinational airframe development and acquisition program. The centerpiece of the JSF program is the Lockheed Martin F-35 Lightning II. The program has been plagued by cost overruns, delays, and performance issues.
170. Vice Admiral John A. Lockard, U.S. Navy (ret.), was commander of Naval Air Systems Command 1995–2000. He joined the Navy in 1964 and flew three combat tours in Vietnam and one in Libya. Lockard was awarded the Distinguished Flying Cross among other commendations and retired from active duty in 2000.
171. Naval Air Systems Command.
172 William Sebastian Cohen (b. August 28, 1940) served as the 20th secretary of defense, 1997–2001. Previously he had been a United States senator from Maine, 1979–1997.

and thank God we do. The Joint Strike Fighter is coming, but it's late and it's challenged and whatever.

But when I left my post, part of my delivery was, "What I see going forward for naval aviation is carrier decks that are manned with F-18 Super Hornets and then Joint Strike Fighters, first a mix, and maybe eventually all Joint Strike Fighters, but that's a long time from now. We've got to have that Super Hornet in there or we're going to be in big trouble." So we have it. It's a magnificent airplane. I got to fly it when I was CNO, backseat, dual control.

I flew two airplanes when I was the CNO. Well, three, actually. One was the Super Hornet down at Pax River. I wanted to fly it because I thought it might help in this debate and argument, and with congressional testimony, and there's nothing like firsthand experience.

JR: Sure.

JJ: So I did. I went down there and flew it from the backseat. It was fabulous. Beautiful airplane. I also flew the V-22 Osprey[173] down there for the same reason, and I made a deal with the commandant,[174] who was not an aviator, that I'd fly the Osprey as well as the Super Hornet so that when we were sitting side by side testifying and somebody

---

173. The Bell Boeing V-22 Osprey is a multi-mission, tilt-rotor aircraft with vertical takeoff and landing (VTOL) and short takeoff and landing (STOL) capabilities. It began operational duty with the U.S. Marine Corps in 2007.
174. The two commandants of the Marine Corps who bridged Admiral Johnson's tenure as CNO were General Charles C. Krulak (July 1, 1995–June 30, 1999) and General James L. Jones (July 1, 1999–January 12, 2003).

would ask a question or raise an issue with the Osprey, having flown it, I might be able to help him.

And then I flew a Gulfstream GV[175] before I left, because we wanted some of those for the Navy. But I didn't want to be viewed as feathering my own nest with that beautiful airplane, so I flew it out of Reagan National,[176] as did the Air Force chief of staff[177] that day, and it helped us get support for those aircraft after I left my post, so I never saw them when I was on active duty. So anyway, I digress. But those were my flying stories from my time as CNO.

The original point was that the F-18 E/F Super Hornet was really important, and we were supported with that program, after much hand-wringing and emotion.

JR: So was your most effective argument in defense of that program, that gap that you identified?

JJ: The gap was a huge part of it and also the capability enhancement. If you saw a Super Hornet fly over right now, you'd go, "Well, there goes an F-18 Hornet." And if 30 minutes from now an F-18C[178] flew over, you'd say, "Well, there goes another one." But if you see them physically sitting side by side, Super Hornet's a much bigger aircraft, and capabilities-wise, it's a very different aircraft on the plus. So it really was a new build, if

---

175. The Gulfstream Aerospace Model GV (G-5) is a fourteen-passenger four-crew long-range business jet. The military designation for the aircraft is C-37A, and it entered service in June 1997. It can reach speeds of Mach 0.90, has a ceiling of 51,000 feet, and a range of 6,500 nautical miles.
176. Ronald Reagan Washington National Airport (KDCA), located in Arlington, Virginia.
177. The three chiefs of staff of the Air Force who bridged Admiral Johnson's tenure as CNO were General Ronald R. Fogleman (October 26, 1994–September 1, 1997), General Ralph E. Eberhart (Acting) (September 2, 1997–October 5, 1997), and General Michael E. Ryan (October 6, 1997–September 5, 2001).
178. The McDonnell Douglas F/A-18 Hornet is a twin-engine supersonic, all-weather carrier-capable multirole combat fighter/attack aircraft introduced in the Navy in 1983. The F/A-18C is a 1987 variant with upgraded radar, avionics, and missile capability.

you will, even though its genesis was obviously the F-18 Hornet. I can't remember what the commonality of parts is. But it's a magnificent airplane and now it's flying for the Navy. It's flying the electronic—it replaced the Prowlers, the electronic warfare aircraft for the United States Navy, and I should know whether the Marines are flying it for their electronic aircraft. I don't think they are yet. Anyway, and internationally.

JR: What about the V-22? That's another controversial program.

JJ: Yeah, very controversial, but I must say—I wasn't sure, to be honest. It's really cool when you take off like a helicopter with your left thumb, push the coolie switch forward on the throttle and then the cells rotate down, and the next thing you know, you're doing 250 knots forward speed. You go, "Wow, that's impressive." [*Laughs*] But I know it had a lot of emotion and concern, and everybody had their views on it, but today, it's everywhere. Not everywhere, but I mean it's elemental to the Marine Corps, the Special Ops folks are using it, Joint Special Ops[179] folks are using it or will start using it, the Navy's going to start using it, I think maybe even for their carrier onboard delivery. But the V-22 has proliferated mightily and, by all reports, is doing very well. So who knew? [*Laughs*]

JR: So that worked out.

JJ: Yeah.

---

179. Joint Special Operations Command (JSOC) is a component command of United States Special Operations Command (USSOCOM) tasked with planning and executing special operations training, exercises, and missions worldwide.

JR: Let's see. There was the issue of integrating women into the force at sea. How big an issue was that? I've got the first women assigned to USS *Eisenhower* in March of '94, which is before you became CNO, but how big an issue was that during your years?

JJ: Well, it was an important issue, it still is, and I said then and I would say now that the integration within the fleet, the success or not of that integration platform by platform, command by command, is still a direct function of leadership. The leadership of that command has to understand it, they have to embrace that reality, and they have to work it. And when they do, it's great. And when they don't, it's not. Gee, guess what? Does that sound like it's always been? Forget the integration of women. How about the integration of new troops, new sailors coming onboard a ship? If the leadership is engaged, if everyone respects everyone else, and everybody understands their mission tasks, it's pretty powerful. When they don't, it's not. So it's still, to me, all of this integration of women and everything attendant to that, it's a commitment and consistent commitment of leadership to that reality that's going to make it work.

JR: It's just like any other leadership challenge.

JJ: I believe so. I'm not trivializing it. It's a big deal, but it's a leadership responsibility to make it work, and there are plenty of them out there that know how to do that and have done it beautifully, male and female, by the way, because they're both in command positions at all levels now. So back to one of my four stars: leadership.

[cell phone interruption; recorder turned off]

JJ: To me, the most important thing to talk about was what we've discussed, which was how I got there and what I did coming into the position, "Steer by the Stars," and then the Super Hornet part was very important to me.

Another aspect of it that I think wasn't my time as CNO, but one of the things that I felt really good about was the importance of senior enlisted leadership, and how elemental that is—I guess it always has been, but how elemental that is to the success of the Navy. When we got command master chief petty officers of the Navy,[180] that really, I thought, was a positive step for us. So the relationships with the MCPONs,[181] the relationships between the service chief and the E10,[182] if you will, the Master Chief Petty Officer of the Navy, was hugely important and that was very helpful in bringing what I talked about before, about kind of the broadcasting, and I mean broadcast as in not telephone broadcast, but just getting the word out and getting the support and the feedback loops. I thought the senior enlisted leadership was magnificent during my time as CNO and so important. There's a lot more structure to it, a lot more depending upon it than perhaps I gave it credit for before I had the CNO experience. I couldn't have done my job without good MCPONs and their staffs and the whole chief's mess, if you will.

---

180. A command master chief petty officer (CMC) is the most senior enlisted sailor in a Navy unit, who reports directly to the commanding officer. The Master Chief Petty Officer of the Navy is the top enlisted sailor, who reports to the CNO.
181. Master Chief Petty Officers of the Navy.
182. The Master Chief Petty Officer of the Navy rank is a special E9 rank sometimes referred to colloquially as E10.

JR: Right. So taking care of the enlisted force was a big part of what you were emphasizing.

JJ: Yes, absolutely, and understanding them and getting that understanding at a level that perhaps I wouldn't have been able to get without the MCPON being there with me. We traveled virtually always together on international trips out to the fleet, not always, but a lot, and the MCPON's perspective on the things that he and I were hearing was extremely helpful to me and not necessarily—he was hearing it differently than I was hearing it in some instances. He had different filters in his head, and it was powerful, on the good side. That relationship was hugely important and I felt very fortunate to have the MCPON as one of my close advisors, but more than that, he was a friend and he was a shipmate of the first order, who was never afraid to tell the boss what needed to be told, good or otherwise.

JR: That's useful.

JJ: Yeah.

JR: So you advocated for food stamp relief for sailors who needed it.

JJ: Honestly, I probably did. I don't recall that. If it was something that would help sailors that needed it at the time, yes.

JR: I remember at the time that was kind of a new thing, but what it really did was highlight the wage problems.

JJ: Yes.

JR: As a way of showing that we needed to take better care of our force.

JJ: Yes.

JR: It was a kind of powerful way to do it.

JJ: Yes.

JR: To say, "If you won't pay our guys what they need to live—."

JJ: Then give them food stamps.

JR: Then give them food stamps.

JJ: Yeah, I do remember that.

JR: I thought that was an effective way to highlight that.

JJ: Yes.

JR: I wanted to back up for a second to "From the Sea,"[183] that concept or construct, the "From the Sea" framework. Were you involved with formulating that? I know during your tenure it was an operative concept.

JJ: Yes.

JR: But when you were at the Strategic Studies Group at the Pentagon, was that something that came out of that? Was it earlier than that?

JJ: You're getting me—first of all, the SSG, the Strategic Studies Group,[184] are you talking about the one I was on?

JR: Yeah.

JJ: That's in Newport, working for the CNO, and that concept I believe did evolve from there. That's my recollection. You could truth-check me on that.[185]

---

183. "... From the Sea: Preparing the Naval Service for the 21st Century" was a September 1992 Navy and Marine Corps white paper that defined a combined vision for the Navy and Marine Corps. It was issued by Secretary of the Navy Sean O'Keefe, Chief of Naval Operations Admiral Frank B. Kelso II, and Commandant of the Marine Corps General C. E. Mundy Jr. It was intended to serve as a post–Cold War successor to the 1980s Maritime Strategy.
184. The Chief of Naval Operations Strategic Studies Group (SSG) was established by Chief of Naval Operations Admiral Thomas B. Hayward in 1981 with the mission to "generate revolutionary naval warfare concepts."
185. In 1991 Secretary of the Navy Sean O'Keefe directed Chief of Naval Operations Admiral Frank B. Kelso II and Commandant of the Marine Corps General C.E. Mundy Jr. to stand up an ad hoc Naval Force Capabilities Planning Effort (NFCPE) to determine a new strategic direction for the sea services. The

JR: That was the OpNav Strategic Studies Group.

JJ: Yes. The SSG has been there for quite some time and, it was a group of, at the time, Navy and Marine officers selected for one year of this study on a project that was important to the CNO, to give him a rendering at the end of your year on whatever it was he asked you to look at. Robin Pirie[186] was the director during my time there, and it was a great experience. But, yes, it birthed a lot of concepts, some of which have become realities in years subsequent, but that was part of "From the Sea."

JR: Okay. Yeah, just asking. You improved the interdeployment training cycle during your period?

JJ: We worked very hard on that, yes, to try to bring more predictability to it and more stability to it, so that you could enhance both the training of the units and the people therein, when the new ones came in and when the old ones flowed out, and also help with the maintenance that was required during an interdeployment training cycle, which is easy to say and hard to do. The Second Fleet and the Third Fleet[187] at the time were the two that did the workups for the battle groups as they were getting ready to deploy, and

---

NFCPE drew from several sources. See Col. Gary Anderson, USMC, "Beyond Mahan," Naval War College, Newport Paper #5, August 1993.

186. Robert B. Pirie Jr. (b. 1933) was a 1955 graduate of the U.S. Naval Academy. He retired as a captain in 1975 and directed the CNO Strategic Studies Group from 1989 to 1992. He served as assistant secretary of the navy (Installations and Environment) from March 1994 to October 2000, under secretary of the navy from 12 October 2000 to 20 January 2001, and acting secretary of the navy January to May 2001.

187. The Third Fleet's area of responsibility is the eastern Pacific Ocean from the American mainland to around the International Date Line. It is headquartered at Naval Base Point Loma, near San Diego, California.

so we had good fleet experience on what our strengths were and what we could do better, and that's where the interdeployment training cycle emphasis really generated at the CNO level, back to the CNO's role of organize, train, and equip.

JR: Was that partly a function of budget cutbacks? The need to have efficiencies in those situations can lead to a lot of innovative thinking.

JJ: Yes, but it's also, to your point, when the budget gets stressed, as it frequently is, the classic example is you defer maintenance on ships, and I think most senior officers view it as you can do that, sure, you can get away with that. But tell me when you're going to fall off the face of the Earth, and nobody can tell you that, because you can cheat on that and defer it and defer it and defer it, and then you've saved yourself x amount of money, and all of a sudden one day you're not going to be able to get under way or something bad is going to happen, and it'll be $25x$ to try to fix it, if you can. So it's a fool's errand to think you can get away with that, and it's been proven for decades, yet we still try to get away with it because of budget shortfalls and so on.

So trying to put rigor and predictability into that process is not something that Jay Johnson invented. Leaders at all levels of the Navy and probably the other services, too, have been trying to deal with that forever, and I know they're still dealing with it today. But it's a hugely important issue. You pay a readiness price big time for that.

So that was an element of this interdeployment training cycle work that we tried to get better control of, and to a certain extent we had measured success, I guess, but you're never there with that, in my experience. You're never there. Why? Because the world around you changes so much so frequently. You can never declare victory.

JR: Right. Yeah, the challenges are changing and the equipment is changing. The sailors are changing.

JJ: Yeah, all the above.

JR: Yes. I can see why that's a big challenge.

JJ: Mm-hmm. It's huge.

JR: You know, that's not the kind of thing people get medals for, but it is so important.

JJ: Yeah.

JR: It's not a glamour thing.

JJ: Yeah. In one aspect, it enables everything else. If you do it right, you're doing it from a position of strength and operational strength, training strength, morale strength, all of the above. If you don't do it right, it's crippling in almost every one of those aspects. And like I say, you get to a point where digging out of that hole is really hard and really expensive, and that's expensive in people's lives and morale and it's expensive to the organization.

JR: What were some of the memorable operations during your period as CNO? I know that we had Operation Desert Fox,[188] for example.

JJ: Yeah.

JR: I don't know if you played a role in that one.

JJ: Well, again, the combatant commanders are responsible for the operations like Desert Fox. Did we help? Sure. It's back to our elemental role, our Title X role to help organize, train, and equip the force. So we helped through our fleet commanders in any way we could. We were involved that way. But the operational aspects of it—I had no control over that. You could say, well, you do sort of because you're a member of the Joint Chiefs of Staff, and that's true, but still, it's the domain of the combatant commander.

JR: So they had a lot of, if not autonomy, they could run it the way they needed to?

JJ: I would hope so, and we were there to help them in any way we could. That's probably a fair way to say it.

---

188. Operation Desert Fox, December 16–19, 1998, was a combined U.S./U.K. punitive bombing campaign against Iraq for noncompliance with United Nations Security Council resolutions and interference with United Nations Special Commission inspectors.

JR: How were relations on the Joint Staff then? A good group of people?

JJ: Yeah, I would say so. My memories of working with Joint Staff were very good ones, and everybody I worked with on the Joint Chiefs of Staff, as you might expect, are still very dear friends today. We each had our service views, probably our service biases, as we talked earlier, and, you know, pounded the table once in a while at each other, but at the end of the day, we knew what had to be done. For the most part, I think we worked very well together to do it. And the Joint Staff was pretty supportive. I can't give you an example of where I was wringing my hands, although I probably did sometimes.

JR: But no significant challenges or breakdowns?

JJ: I don't recall any breakdowns, no.

JR: It seems like the late nineties was a period when things were working pretty well.

JJ: Well, yeah. I guess you could say it depends on who you talk to, because they were worried that the procurement budget had been going down. Admiral Bill Owens,[189] when he was the vice chairman, worked very hard to try to redirect that curve back to the positive, and it happened over time. I think we worked very hard on getting the budget support on the personnel side and other sides turned around. We redirected the curve, let's put it that way, in the later years.

---

189. Admiral William A. "Bill" Owens, U.S. Navy (ret.) (b. May 8, 1940) served as vice chairman of the Joint Chiefs of Staff 1994–1996.

JR: Was there a sense at the time, thinking strategically, a sense of a foreshadowing of what was to come, a sense that the optimism of the previous post–Cold War period, like there weren't any big challenges anymore, a series of small challenges? Was there any sort of sense that this wasn't going to last long, that things might get more difficult in the future?

JJ: Well, I think the sense is one that is historical. To say "Olly, olly, in [*sic*] free," and "Life is good from this moment forward. Let's just not worry about this stuff anymore," is naïve in the extreme, and history tells you that. So fighting that feeling and being pragmatists, historically based pragmatists, I think was very important. Still is, by the way. A lot of people say, "Well, you don't need the big Army anymore because we're never going to do this mass—." In my time at General Dynamics,[190] we built the M1A2 Abrams[191] main battle tank. Every time we'd get through a conference, they'd say, "Okay, that's it. We're never going to need the tank anymore, so save all that money." Guess what? Wrong answer. [*Laughs*]

So it's a reality that I think military professionals need to give balance to with Congress, a Congress that's not proliferated with a lot of military experience, although there are some really good members of Congress now who have lots of military experience, Navy SEALs[192] and so forth. But in big numbers, in percentages, it's still

---

190. General Dynamics Corporation is an aerospace and defense multinational corporation headquartered in West Falls Church, Virginia.
191. The M1A2 is an advanced version of the M1 Abrams main battle tank. It entered service in 1992 and is expected to remain part of the force until the mid-twenty-first century.
192. The U.S. Navy "Sea, Air, and Land" (SEAL) teams are the Navy's primary special operations force and a component of the Naval Special Warfare Command.

very low. We lost the World War II generation in Congress, for example. So I think this idea that life as we know it is going to be good now, all you have to do is read the paper, it's a really dangerous world out there, and we need to stay prepared and we need the best fighting force in the world, and anybody who thinks we don't is a simpleton, in my view.

JR: I can guess that when you were making the argument for the Super Hornet, one of the questions you faced was, "Well, why do we need all that?"

JJ: That's what you always face. "Why do we need new aircraft carriers?"

"They're antiques."

"No, they're not."

As long as I will be on this Earth and well beyond, I still will believe that the ability to generate combat power from the sea is elemental at a national strategic level, and there's nothing that does it like a 98- or 100,000-ton nuclear aircraft carrier. And having that kit in your strategic arsenal is one of the things that differentiates America from anybody else. If you don't believe that, just look around and see who's building aircraft carriers to try to say, "Me too."

JR: Yeah, China.

JJ: Yeah. So, anyway, you get the point.

JR: Well, I can remember the debate particularly from when you were CNO, of folks saying, "Blue water is not as important anymore."

JJ: Sure.

JR: "We're green- and brown-water-capable. Why would we focus on building big ships?"

JJ: That's exactly right. Because 90-what-percentage of global commerce moves by sea, and having sea lanes open and available to move that commerce is pretty elemental to global economic stability. I don't think that's changed since I retired, and I don't think it's going to change anytime soon. So do we have a global responsibility there? In my opinion, absolutely. And believe it or not, the world is dependent on the United States Navy in that role for a long time, and we see that at our national strategic peril.

JR: Right. So when I have heard folks say that, you know, Mahan's[193] world view of the decisive nature of fleets is passé or it doesn't matter anymore, things like that—

JJ: My answer to that: that's bullshit. [*Laughs*] Okay?

JR: Simply said. [*Laughs*]

---

193. Alfred Thayer Mahan (September 27, 1840–December 1, 1914) was a Navy officer and naval theorist who served as a lecturer and president of the Naval War College. His *The Influence of Sea Power upon History, 1660–1783* (1890) is a seminal work of naval strategy that was greatly influential in the development of American naval power. Mahan emphasized the primacy of capital ships and controlling seaborne commerce.

JJ: Yeah. That's a view expressed by someone who really doesn't understand.

JR: I've always thought it was a consequence of success. If you're the only fleet left standing after World War II, essentially; I mean, the Russians had something, but not serious, people can think, "Oh, it doesn't matter," because they don't know how much it does matter if we had a competitor.

JJ: That's exactly right. You tend to take that stuff for granted and then it loses importance to you and you're off on another tangent. But I think, again back to the role of military professionals, you can't let it be taken for granted, and the message has to be rearticulated, reinforced, reaffirmed, and that's not easy, but it's hugely important, and there are no better people to do that than the military professionals.

JR: The example I would use when teaching about this was when we look at a map of the world and look at the oceans, we look at places we can go, essentially. That's our view of the world, that we can go anywhere we want.

JJ: Yeah.

JR: But what if one day we woke up and there was a Chinese aircraft carrier off the coast of Cuba? How would we feel about that?

JJ: Mm-hmm. And one day there will be.

JR: It's, unfortunately, true.

JJ: Yeah. This idea of ship numbers and ship capabilities—did we talk about that the last time?

JR: Only a little. We can talk more about it.

JJ: It's interesting. Presence really matters, and there are people who don't agree with that, but my experience throughout my Navy career and beyond makes me very much believe that presence matters. It matters to our allies, it matters to the world. Whether you're a good guy or a bad guy, it really matters. And in order to have presence, you have to have ships, and you can get into this interesting discussion about technology and the fact that technology really is going to allow us to buy fewer ships and do this. Okay, that's one view. My view is that—and I've said this for probably almost twenty years now—that technology's a wonderful thing, but we still haven't figured out—technology hasn't allowed us to put one ship in two places at the same time. So numbers really do matter.

The other way to say it is that virtual presence is actual absence, and to an ally who's counting on the United States Navy to be there, knowing that there's a carrier battle group—you pick the range—50 miles, 100 miles from my shore, ready to help me, makes all the difference in the world, and they don't have to have anybody's permission to be there. So I believe that ship numbers and capabilities really do matter, and that's an issue that's been ongoing forever. It's ongoing right now as we have to rebuild or replace the strategic submarine fleet while we build more attack submarines to replace the ones that are retiring. So, anyway, I digress.

JR: No, that's important stuff. It was important when you were in command.

JJ: Yeah.

JR: Still important today. I think that continuity aspect of types of challenges is important for people to know, because every ten or twenty years or so you get people saying, "Everything has changed. The fundamentals no longer apply. You know, it was revolutionary times," and things like this.

JJ: You're exactly right. Guess what? They're still there. [*Laughs*]

JR: Then something will happen to prove that that's not the case.

JJ: Yeah.

JR: Were there any other challenges or circumstances of your time as CNO that would be useful for folks to know? We covered a lot of points on that, but if there's anything else that—

JJ: I think we hit the big ones, to be honest with you, kind of the unique way I got appointed to be the CNO. I will say my service as the CNO the last four years of my career was the greatest privilege of service in my life. I didn't anticipate it, but I treasure it and did the best I could with it. But people ask, "Don't you miss it?"

And my answer is, "No."

And they look at me like, "Wow! What's wrong with you?"

I say, "Wait a minute. Wise men once told me," back to Stan Arthur and other mentors like that, "that there'll come a time when it's not your turn anymore, and you can spend the rest of your life wishing you were still the CNO or a four-star admiral or a twenty-eight-year-old Navy fighter pilot flying fighters off of carrier decks, all interesting, but it's not your turn anymore."

So as I retired, I got my head around that and I decided I would not spend the rest of my life wishing I were still in the Navy, and it doesn't take anything away from my time in the Navy. I had an unbelievable career, the greatest privilege of my life, as I told you, but what I've done is I took that thirty-two-and-a-half-year, or whatever it was, Navy career and put it in a lockbox, treasure chest, and put it on the shelf. And back to my "Steer by the stars that are out ahead of you instead of the wake that's behind you," I'm steering by new stars. But I've got that treasure chest of Navy that nobody can ever take away from me, and anytime I want to open it up and relive part of it or think about it or whatever, celebrate it, bitch about it, whatever it might be, it's mine to do. Nobody can touch it. But it's time to move forward.

I've told every CNO since then, kind of like Colin Powell told me, "Hey, it's not my turn anymore. I'm always here for whatever you need, but I'll never get in your way and you'll never, ever hear me or read about me complaining about something the Navy's doing. I'll never do that." So that's where I am.

JR: I guess that's true in any career, though, that you make those transitions periodically, even [unclear].

JJ: Indeed you do.

JR: From being more tactically oriented to having operational-level commander to—

JJ: I remember Paul David Miller,[194] who's a dear friend and another great mentor. Admiral Miller told me, when he was CinCLant and I was the battle group commander as a one-star at Carrier Group 8,[195] he said in one of our conversations something like, "This would be the last time you'll—." I forget how he said it, but basically it was where you'll know everybody on your team up close and personal and that you'll have them very close to you. That's really not the way he said it, but the point was, the scale of where you're going from now on is so great that it's going to demand a different kind of leadership. That doesn't take anything away from the personal aspects of it, but delegation and that will be much more important as you move to your next few posts within the Navy. I

---

194. Admiral Paul David Miller, U.S. Navy (ret.) (b. December 1, 1941) served 1964–1994, and at the time of his retirement was commander in chief, U.S. Atlantic Command.
195. Carrier Group 8 is currently Carrier Strike Group 8, stationed at Norfolk, Virginia.

thought it was a very interesting point and very true. It's the last time you feel like you've got control of everything. [*Laughs*]

JR: Right. I heard the expression once, "hand con."

JJ: Yeah, exactly.

JR: Shake hands and you know it's going to happen.

JJ: Exactly.

JR: You go above that, you can't look the guy in the eye the same way.

JJ: Yeah. Very true.

JR: So I guess you've also played a mentorship role for various officers over the years, people who've come up with the same problems, giving guidance.

JJ: I try, yeah, and I talk to retiring officers now about that transition in the context of what we've already talked about, "It's not your turn anymore, and that's okay. Not a bad thing. But you've got to decide what do you want to do for the rest of your life. Do you want to consult? Do you want to work full-time? Do you want to go nonprofit? Whatever it is you want, take some time when you retire to sort that out, and then once you do, go." I went into business, had business opportunities, and it's been a wonderful experience.

JR: Dominion Resources, Dominion Energy.[196]

JJ: And it's been a great experience, but once you commit to something like that, working full-time, you don't spend as much time doing Navy changes of command, Navy speeches, that kind of thing that perhaps some of your shipmates would expect you to do. But again, it's a career transition and it's okay.

JR: And there are still ways to serve.

JJ: Absolutely. I'm on the Naval Academy Foundation[197] board right now, so, yeah.

JR: Is there anything else you'd like to add at this point in the game?

JJ: I don't think so. I appreciate the opportunity and I treasured my time in the Navy, as I've told you. It was the greatest privilege of service in my life. I think that's a good way to end it.

JR: A great story. [*Laughs*]

---

196. Dominion Energy, Inc., is a power and energy company headquartered in Richmond, Virginia.
197. The U.S. Naval Academy Foundation mission is to "help to advance the Naval Academy and the Naval Academy Alumni Association by providing private resources to achieve and maintain a broad range of mission-enhancing activities that support the nation's premier leadership institution and its graduates."

[End of March 21, 2016 interview]

Personal Data

Born: June 5, 1946, Great Falls, Montana
Spouse: Garland Hawthorne (1947–2013), m. 1969–2011 (divorced)
Sydney "Nini" Ferguson m. 2011–
Children: Cullen Johnson Hill, daughter, b. 1971; m. Noah M. Hill
Grandchildren: Noah Hawthorne Hill, b. 2013
Education: 1968: U.S. Naval Academy
1976: Armed Forces Staff College
1990: Naval War College Strategic Studies Group

Medals and Awards in order of precedence

Defense Distinguished Service Medal
Navy Distinguished Service Medal
Defense Superior Service Medal
Legion of Merit with 3 gold award stars
Defense Meritorious Service Medal
Meritorious Service Medal
Air Medal with bronze strike/flight numeral 8
Navy and Marine Corps Commendation Medal
Navy Unit Commendation
Navy Meritorious Unit Commendation with 2 bronze service stars
Navy Expeditionary Medal
National Defense Service Medal with 1 service star
Armed Forces Expeditionary Medal with 1 service star
Vietnam Service Medal with 2 service stars
Southwest Asia Service Medal with 1 service star
Armed Forces Service Medal
Navy Sea Service Deployment Ribbon with 6 service stars
Vietnam Gallantry Cross with bronze star
Armed Forces Honor Medal, 1st class (Vietnam)
Order of National Security Merit, Tong-il Medal (Republic of Korea)
NATO Medal for Former Yugoslavia
Vietnam Campaign Medal
Kuwait Liberation Medal (Kuwait)
Navy Marksmanship Ribbon for Rifle

Non-military: Distinguished Eagle Scout Award

Summary and Keywords

The main points of interest in this interview are:
Naval Academy life in the 1960s
Vietnam War carrier flight operations

Operations in the Mediterranean in the 1980s, and in particular strikes on Libya in 1986 (Operation El Dorado Canyon)
The Tailhook Scandal
Development and employment of Joint capabilities in the 1990s
Operation Uphold Democracy (Haiti 1994–1995)
Development of the F/A-18E and F/A-18F Super Hornet
Suicide of Adm. Jeremy Boorda
Leadership concepts
Perspectives on service life

Keywords:
Adm. Jeremy Boorda
Boy Scouts of America
Carrier Flight operations
Chief of Naval Operations
Command Master Chief Petty Officers of the Navy
F/A-18E and F/A-18F Super Hornet
Flight training
Haiti
Jointness
Libya
Navy Leadership
Operation El Dorado Canyon
Operation Uphold Democracy
Special MAGTF
Steer by the Stars
Super-CAG
Tailhook
U.S. Naval Academy
USNA Class of 1968
Vietnam War

Launched in 1969, the U.S. Naval Institute's award-winning oral history program is among the oldest in the country. Used in combination with documentary sources, oral histories offer a richer understanding of naval history through candid recollections and explanations rarely entered into contemporary records. In addition, they help depict the atmosphere of a particular event or era in a manner not available in official documents.

The nonprofit Naval Institute accomplishes its history projects through contributed funds and gratefully accepts tax-deductible gifts of all sizes for this purpose. This support allows the Institute to preserve the life experiences of today's service men and women so they may enlighten and inspire future generations.

For information about opportunities to underwrite Naval Institute oral history projects, please contact the Naval Institute Foundation at 291 Wood Road, Annapolis, Maryland 21402; by phone at (410) 295-1054; or by e-mail at foundation@usni.org.

Index to the Oral History of Adm. Jay L. Johnson, USN (Ret.)

A-6 Intruder aircraft, 17, 17n39, 20, 22
A-7/A-7E Corsair II, 25, 25n61, 51–54
Adams, Eddie, 29n64, 31
Adaptive Joint Force Package concept, 80n133
advancements and demands for different kind of leadership, 127–28
Air Force Academy, U.S.: application to attend, 5; founding of and first graduating class at, 5, 5n15; interest in attending after seeing Thunderbirds performance, 5; location of, 5; tour of during National Jamboree, 5
Air Force Memorial, U.S., 33, 33n71
Air Force, U.S.: AFSC training, 63; El Dorado Canyon operation, 50–54; formation of, 2n4; longest fighter combat mission, 52, 52n94; Tactical Fighter Wing, 20th, 52n94; Tactical Fighter Wing, 48th, 52n94
Airborne Corps, XVIII, 80n131, 81, 81n136
aircraft carriers: aspiration to command a carrier, 56; designations for, 76, 76n125; escort of Soviet bombers from, 35–37; Marines deployment on, 70–71, 70n117, 75–79, 76n124, 86; procurement budget and justification for, 121–22; readiness and alert conditions on, 35; Super CAG Program and coequal command of air group and aircraft carrier, 54–57, 54n96. *See also* naval aviation/carrier aviation
airline jobs, 39, 40
Alameda Naval Air Station, 40, 40n79
America, 51, 51n91, 80, 80n132, 86
Anderson, James "Luca," 47n86
Aristide, Jean-Bertrand, 79n129, 83n139
Arizona, 98n157
Arlington National Cemetery, 32, 33n70
Armed Forces Staff College (AFSC)/Joint Forces Staff College (JFSC), 60–63, 60n106
Army, U.S.: AFSC training, 63; Airborne Corps, XVIII, 80n131, 81, 81n136; Special Operations Aviation Regiment, 160th, 80, 80nn133–134, 86; Uphold Democracy operation, 80–81, 80n131, 80nn133–134, 84–87
Army Air Corps, U.S.: 8th Air Force, 2, 2n5; establishment and successor of, 2n4
Army Air Forces, U.S., 2n4
Arthur, Stanley R. "Stan," 99–100, 99n160, 126
Attack Squadron 155, 25
aviation and flying: fighter pilot aspirations, 100–101; first airplane trip, 8; first time in military jet, 17; flight training, 16–17, 17nn37–40, 19–20, 19nn45–49; interest in after seeing Thunderbirds performance, 5, 7; wings, awarding of, 19

B-24 Liberator, 2, 2n2
Badlands, 4, 4n11
Barrow, John Curtis, 26–28, 26n62, 45
Bausell, 18, 18n42
Bausell, Lewis K., 18n42
Bay Lop (Nguyen Van Lém), 29n64, 31
Bear bombers, 35–37, 35n75

Bell Boeing V-22 Osprey aircraft, 107–8, 107n173, 109
Benghazi, 49–54
Berlin LaBelle disco bombing, 49–50, 49n88
Bishop, Maurice, 85n145
Black Forest, Colorado Springs, 4–6, 4n10
Blair, Dennis C. "Denny," 13, 13n27
Boeing F/A-18E and F/A-18F Super Hornet aircraft, 106–7, 106n168, 108–9, 111, 121
Boorda, Jeremy Michael "Mike," 92–95, 92n148, 102–3
Borah, Daniel Vernor, Jr. "Dazzle," 25, 25n60
Bowman, Frank Lee "Skip," 93, 93n149
Boy Scouts of America (BSA): Distinguished Eagle Scout Award, 3, 3n9; Eagle Scout rank, 3n8; Eagle Scout rank and effect of Scouting on life, 3–7, 3nn8–9; monument at Briargate to commemorate the Jamboree, 6; National Jamboree, Colorado Springs, 4–6, 4nn10–14
Broadmoor resort, 21, 21n55
Bronstein, 10n22
Brown, Doug, 80, 80n134, 86
Bryant, Stanley W., "Stan," 71–72, 71n118
Bureau of Naval Personnel (BuPers), 28, 31–33, 32n69, 55–56, 58, 60
Bush, George Herbert Walker, 100, 100n161
Bush, George Walker, 84, 84n141

C-37A aircraft, 108n175
Calvert, James Francis "Jim," 12, 12n24
Cannibal Queen (Coonts), 21–22
career in Navy: Armed Forces Staff College, 60–63, 60n106; aspiration to command a carrier, 56; Bureau of Naval Personnel, 28, 31–33, 32n69, 55–56, 58, 60; Carrier Air Wing One command, 46–54, 46n82, 58; Carrier Air Wing One Super CAG Program, 54–57, 54n96, 58; Carrier Group 8 command, 70–72, 70n111, 75–79, 127; decision to stay in Navy, 39–42, 100–101; education opportunities that didn't work out, 63; flag officer, selection for, 57, 58; as greatest privilege in life, 126, 129; lieutenant commander, early selection for, 41; mentors and other supportive senior leaders, 97–98, 97nn154–155, 98nn156–158, 99–101, 99nn159–160, 100n161, 126–28; most important things about, 111–12; Naval War College, Strategic Studies Group, 57–60, 57nn99–100, 58n101, 59n103, 114–15, 114n184, 115n186; O-6 command screening, 55; Second Fleet command, 79–87; ship qualifications, work to complete, 56; Sixth Fleet operations officer, 55, 56, 58; Special Ops fastboat trip to *Mount Whitney*, 86–87; VF-84 squadron command, 42–44, 42n80, 46, 58; VF-101 squadron, 38–39, 38n77; VF-142 squadron, 34–37, 34n73; VF-191 squadron, 22–27. See also Chief of Naval Operations; *Oriskany*
Carrier Air Wing One (CAG-1): command of, 46–54, 46n82, 58; Super CAG Program and command of, 54–57, 54n96, 58
Carrier Group 8 command, 70–72, 70n111, 75–79, 127
Carter, Walter E., Jr. "Ted," 16, 16n35
Cédras, Joseph Raoul, 79n129, 83, 83n139
Chief of Naval Operations: acting CNO assignment, 92, 94–95; Boorda as and suicide of Boorda, 92–95, 92n148, 102–3; challenges faced as, 101–3, 119–25; confirmation as

and round-the-world tour, 96, 98–99; nomination as CNO, 95–98; operations during time as, 118, 118n188; privilege to serve as, 126, 129; responsibilities of, 103–10, 103n166, 118; "Steer by the Stars" vision statement, 96, 96n153, 99, 103, 111; support from senior officers during time as, 97, 97nn154–155, 99–101, 99nn159–160

Clinton, William Jefferson "Bill," 84, 84n140, 94–95, 102n164
Cohen, Jay Martin, 13, 13n33
Cohen, William Sebastian "Bill," 106, 106n172
Cold War: activities during, 37–38; escort of Soviet bombers, 35–37; relevance of, 37–38
Colorado Springs, Boy Scout National Jamboree at, 4–6, 4nn10–14
command master chief petty officer (CMC), 111, 111n180
Congress members, military experience of, 120–21
Consolidated B-24 Liberator, 2, 2n2
Coonts, Stephen "Steve," 20–22, 20n50
Coral Sea, 51, 51n92, 53, 57
Coral Sea, Battle of the, 51n92
Corpus Christi Naval Air Station, 19, 19n49
Cosgrove, Bill, 12
Covey, Richard O. "Dick," 6, 6n17

Dasault Mirage aircraft, 47n84, 47n85
DC-3 aircraft, 8, 8n19
DeMars, Bruce, 97, 97n154
Denton, Jeremiah Andrew, Jr., 60–61, 60n107
Desert Fox, Operation, 118n188
Desert Storm, Operation, 75, 76n121
Distinguished Flying Cross, 26n62, 38n78, 71n118, 100n161, 102n163, 106n170
Distinguished Service Cross, 102n164
Dominican Republic, 82, 82n138
Dominion Energy, Inc, 129, 129n196
Dougherty, Francis J. "Bud," 38, 38n78
Douglas DC-3 aircraft, 8, 8n19
Douglass, John W., 93, 93n150
Dwight D Eisenhower "Ike," 35, 35n74, 110

Easter Offensive, 24, 24n59
Eberhart, Ralph E., 108n177
Eddie Adams: Saigon '68, 31
Eisenhower, Dwight D., 4, 4n13
El Dorado Canyon, Operation, 48–54, 48n87, 49n88, 57, 58
enlisted senior leadership, important of, 111–12, 111nn180–182
Enterprise, 20, 21n52

F-4 Phantom II aircraft, 17, 17n38, 23
F-8/F-8J Crusader aircraft, 20n51, 23–24, 23n56, 33, 34
F-14 Tomcat aircraft, 33–34, 33n72, 38, 53, 60, 106n168
F-35 Lightning II aircraft, 106n169

F-100C Super Sabre aircraft, 5n16
F-111 Aardvark aircraft, 51–54, 51n93
F/A-18 and F/A-18C Hornet aircraft, 106n168, 108–9, 108n178
F/A-18E and F/A-18F Super Hornet aircraft, 106–7, 106n168, 108–9, 111, 121
Fighter Squadron VF-84 Jolly Rogers, 42–44, 42n80, 46, 58
Fighter Squadron VF-101 Grim Reapers, 38–39, 38n77
Fighter Squadron VF-142 Ghostriders, 34–37, 34n73
Fighter Squadron VF-191 Hellcats, 22–27
Final Countdown, The, 43, 43b81
Flight of the Intruder (Coonts), 20
flight training: Coonts as classmate during, 20–22, 20n50; F-14 Tomcat training, 33, 60; impressions of, 19–20; length of time to complete, 19; locations of training, 19, 19nn45–46, 19nn48–49, 33; summer program preparations for, 16–17, 17nn37–40
Foggy Bottom, 95–96, 96n152
Fogleman, Ronald R., 108n177
food stamp relief for sailors, 112–14
Forrestal, 18, 18n43, 102n165
Forrestal, James, 18n43, 101n162
Forrestal Lectures, 101, 101n162
forward presence, 124–25
Froaker, Swede, 19

Gaddafi, Muammar, 47n84, 52, 53
Gaffney, Paul G., II, 13–14, 13n32
General Dynamics F-111 Aardvark aircraft, 51–54, 51n93
General Dynamics M1A2 Abrams tank, 120, 120nn190–191
global responsibilities and capabilities of military services, 122–24
Golden Gate Bridge, 40
Goldwater-Nichols Department of Defense Reorganization Act, 85n143, 104–5, 104n167
Great Falls Air Force Base (Malmstrom Air Force Base), 2, 2n3
Great Falls, Montana, 1–2
Grenada, 85, 85nn144–145
Grumman A-6 Intruder aircraft, 17, 17n39, 20, 22
Grumman F-14 Tomcat aircraft, 33–34, 33n72, 38, 53, 60, 106n168
Gulfstream Aerospace Model GV (G-5) aircraft, 108, 108n175

Hagee, Michael William "Mike," 13, 13n28
Haiti: Cité Soleil, 85, 85n142; follow-through on aid to, 84; goodness of Haitian people, 81, 85; invasion plan and waiving off invasion operation, 82–84, 83n139; joint operations lessons from, 85–87; location and characteristics of, 82, 82n138; Special Ops fastboat trip to *Mount Whitney*, 86–87; stabilization operations in, 84–85; Uphold Democracy operation, 79–87, 79nn128–129, 80n131
hand con, 128
Hayward, Thomas B., 57n100, 114n184
Hispaniola, 82n138
Hogg, James Robert "Jim," 59, 59n103

Holloway, James Lemuel, III "Jim," 98, 98n156, 100
Holloway, James Lemuel, Jr., 98n156

Influence of Sea Power upon History, 1660-1783 (Mahan), 122
Inouye, Daniel Ken "Dan," 102, 102n164
interdeployment training cycle, 115–18
Iraq, 75, 76n121, 118n188

Jefferson, Thomas, 4n12
Johnson, Jay L.: aspiration to be a doctor, 9; attitude of family toward Navy career, 41–42; birth and early life of, 1–7; career decision to stay in Navy, 39–42, 100–101; family of, 41–42; mentor role of, 126–29; Naval Academy experience of, 8–14; Navy career as greatest privilege in life, 126, 129; retirement of, 126, 128–29; transitions, attitude toward, 126–29
Joint Forces Staff College (JFSC)/Armed Forces Staff College (AFSC), 60–63, 60n106
joint operations/jointness: act to create cross-service coordination, 85n143; Armed Forces Staff College/Joint Forces Staff College training for, 60–63, 60n106; attitude toward jointness in general, 87–92; concept of jointness, 85n143; dilution of services in name of jointness, 89–90; El Dorado Canyon operation, 48–54, 48n87, 49n88, 57, 58; issues related to jointness as CNO, 63; joint service academy, 88–89; leadership and success of, 87; Marines deployment on carriers, 70–71, 70n117, 75–79, 76n124, 86; operational usefulness of, 90–91; Uphold Democracy joint operations lessons, 85–87; Uphold Democracy operation, 80–81, 80n131, 80nn133–134; Urgent Fury operation, 85, 85nn143–145
Joint Professional Military Education (JPME) and JPME Phase Two, 61–62, 61n108
Joint Special Operations Command (JSOC), 109, 109n179
Joint Strike Fighter (JSF), 106–7, 106n169
Joint Task Force 120 (JTF-120), 79–87, 79n128
Jones, James L., 107n174

Kauffman, Draper Laurence, 12, 12n23
Kelly, John Patrick, 12, 12n25
Kelly, Raymond Walter "Ray," 81, 81n137
Kelso, Frank Benton, II, 50, 50n90, 71–72, 114n183, 114–15n185
Kidd, Isaac C., 98n157
Kidd, Isaac Campbell, Jr., 98, 98n157
Kingsville Naval Air Station, 19, 19n48
Kinney, Sheldon Hoard, 10–11, 10nn21–22, 27
Kleemann, Henry "Hank," 47, 47n86
Krulak, Charles Chandler "Chuck," 74, 74n119, 107n174
Krulak, Victor H. "Brute," 74n119

LaBelle disco bombing, 49–50, 49n88
Le Trois Continents pizza place, 28–29, 29n65, 31
leadership. *See* officers and leadership
Lehman, John Francis, Jr., 54n96, 56, 56n98

Lém, Nguyen Van (Bay Lop), 29n64, 31
Libya: El Dorado Canyon operation, 48–54, 48n87, 49n88, 57, 58; Gulf of Sidra operations, 46, 46n83; line of death and Gulf of Sidra incident, 47–48, 47nn84–86; longest fighter combat mission, 52, 52n94
life, speed of and don't waste a minute of, 101
Lincoln, Abraham, 4n12
line of death and Gulf of Sidra incident, 47–48, 47nn84–86
Ling-Temco-Vought A-7/A-7E Corsair II, 25, 25n61, 51–54
Loan, Nguyen Ngoc, 28–31, 29nn64–65
Lockard, John A., 106, 106n170
Lockheed Martin F-35 Lightning II aircraft, 106n169

M1A2 Abrams tank, 120, 120nn190–191
Mahan, Alfred Thayer, 122, 122n193
Malmstrom, Einar Axel, 2n2
Malmstrom Air Force Base (Great Falls Air Force Base), 2, 2n3
marathons, 73–74
Marine Corps Marathon, 73–74
Marine Corps, U.S.: AFSC training, 63; classmates who served in, 13nn28–30; Haiti operations, 81; Marine Air-Ground Task Force (MAGTF)/Special MAGTF, 70–71, 70n117, 75–79, 76n124, 86; Vietnam War operations, 9
Master Chief Petty Officers of the Navy (MCPONs), 111–12, 111nn180–182
Mauz, Henry H., Jr. "Hank," 70, 70n115
McCain, John Sidney, III, 102, 102n165
McCain, John Sidney, Jr. "Jack," 102n165
McDonnell Douglas F-4 Phantom II aircraft, 17, 17n38, 23
McDonnell Douglas F/A-18 and F/A-18C Hornet aircraft, 106n168, 108–9, 108n178
McGrail, Charles Reynolds, Jr. "Chuck," 98, 98n158
Medal of Honor, 18n42, 102n164
Mediterranean Sea: El Dorado Canyon operation, 48–54, 48n87, 49n88, 57, 58; Gulf of Sidra operations, 46, 46n83; line of death and Gulf of Sidra incident, 47–48, 47nn84–86; VF-142 deployment, 34–37
Meridian Naval Air Station, 19, 19n46
Meritorious Service medal, 38n78
MiG (Mikoyan-and-Gurevich Design Bureau) aircraft, 23, 23n57
Military Academy, U.S. (West Point), 3, 3n6
military service: anti-military attitudes during Vietnam War, 39–40; Congress members, military experience of, 120–21; family history of military service, 2–3; father's military service, 2–3, 2nn2–5
military services: act to create cross-service coordination, 85n143; dilution of in name of jointness, 89–90; ethos within services as great strengths, 89; global responsibilities and capabilities of, 122–24; inter-service rivalry and jointness, 85n143; joint service academy, 88–89; morale aspect of service rivalries, 91–92; purple to designate joint commands and billets, 89, 89n147; service-specific leadership roles, 88, 90; synergy from differences in services, 90–92. See also joint operations/jointness; *specific services*

Miller, Paul David, 70, 70n113, 76, 76n122, 78, 127–28, 127n194
Mirage aircraft, 47, 47n85
Miramar Naval Air Station, 33, 60
Moore, Charles W. "Willy," Jr, 13, 13n31
Moranville, Kendall E. "Ken," 56, 56n97
Mount Rushmore National Memorial, 4, 4n12
Mount Whitney, 79–80, 80n130, 82, 86
Muczynski, Lawrence "Music," 47n86
Mullen, Michael Glenn "Mike," 13, 13n26
Mundy, C. E., Jr., 114n183, 114–15n185

National Defense University (NDU), 13n32, 14
National Eagle Scout Association, 3n9
Naval Academy Alumni Association, 129n197
Naval Academy Foundation, U.S., 14, 16, 129, 129n197
Naval Academy, U.S.: appointment to, 5; athletics at, 10; commandant of midshipmen st, 10–11, 10nn21–22; comparison of academy then and now, 14–16; discipline, intensity, and focus at, 9–10; distinguished classmates, 12–14, 13nn26–33; feelings about time at and pride in contributions of class, 8–14; first impressions of, 8; Forrestal Lectures, 101, 101n162; impressive abilities and focus of current midshipmen, 14–16; interest in naval aviation and appointment to, 5, 7; knee injury from squaring corner, 10; lifelong bonds built during time in, 8; location of, 3n7; pride in, 14–16; superintendents at, 12, 12nn23–24, 13n31, 16, 16nn35–36; Walberg appointment to and interest in attending, 7; women at, 14
naval aviation/carrier aviation: career terminations and price paid for Tailhook scandal, 66–69; carrier qualifications, 19; communication with Soviet pilots, 36; escort of Soviet bombers, 35–37; fighter pilot aspirations, 100–101; first-class cruise and interest in carrier operations, 17–18, 17n41; interest in and appointment to Naval Academy, 5, 7; readiness and alert conditions on carriers, 35; risk profile of carrier aviator, 24–25; Vietnam War operations, 9
Naval Force Capabilities Planning Effort (NFCPE), 114–15n185
naval presence, 124–25
Naval War College, Strategic Studies Group (SSG), 57–60, 57nn99–100, 58n101, 59n103, 114–15, 114n184, 115n186
Navy, U.S.: attitude about career in, 7, 39; Boorda as sailor's sailor, 94, 95; Boorda suicide, impact of on, 94, 95; Boorda suicide, recovery of Navy after, 99; budget cutbacks, effect of, 116; chain of command, reinforcement of, 102–3; diversity in force, out of phase with time, and culture shift in, 65, 66, 68; enlisted force, taking care of, 111–12; food stamp relief for sailors, 112–14; morale at end of Vietnam war, 39; new CNO, adjustment to, 101–3; procurement budget and justification for capabilities, 119–25; readiness and interdeployment training cycle, 115–18; SEAL predecessors, 12, 12n23; "Steer by the Stars" vision statement, 96, 96n153, 99, 103, 111; underwater demolition team, first, 12, 12n23; women in force at sea, integration of, 110. *See also* career in Navy
Navy and Marine Corps Medal for Heroism, 10n22
Navy Annex, 32, 32n69

Navy Commendation medal, 38n78
Navy Cross, 10n22, 11, 13n29
Nellis Air Force Base, 5n16
Nimitz: Coonts service aboard, 21; development of, 98n156; service history of, 21n54; shakedown cruise on, 35; VF-84 squadron command on, 42–44, 42n80
Nimitz, Chester W., 21n54
Nolan, Bob, 4n14
North, Oliver L. "Ollie," 13, 13n30
North American Rockwell OV-10 Bronco aircraft, 17, 17n40
North American T-2 Buckeye aircraft, 19, 19n47

Oceana Naval Air Station, 28, 28n63, 33–34, 46n82
officers and leadership: advancements and demands for different kind of leadership, 127–28; chain of command, reinforcement of, 102–3; challenges of commanding a squadron, 43–44; decisions and preparations for becoming a career naval officer, 39, 100–101; delegation and trust, importance of, 44–45, 127–28; enlisted senior leadership, important of, 111–12, 111nn180–182; flag officer, eligibility for, 57; influence of and impressive leadership of Barrow, 26–28, 26n62, 45; joint operations success, leadership role in, 87; lessons from senior officers, 45–46; mentors and other supportive senior leaders, 97–98, 97nn154–155, 98nn156–158, 99–101, 99nn159–160, 100n161, 126–28; officers of integrity, 27; realities of being a commanding officer, 43–45; respectful relationships and earning respect, 44, 110; Super CAG Program and coequal command of air group and aircraft carrier, 54–57, 54n96; tell people what you want and let them do their job, 45; women in force at sea, responsibility for integration of, 110
O'Keefe, Sean, 114n183, 114–15n185
Oriskany: anti-military activities toward, 40; assignment to, 21; Barrow as commanding office on, 26–28, 26n62; loss of men on, 24–25, 25n60; morale aboard, 25–27; service history of, 21n53; smoking policy aboard, 72–73; Vietnam War combat cruises on, 22–28, 25n60
Oriskany, Battle of, 21n53
Osley, Buzz, 17
OV-10 Bronco aircraft, 17, 17n40
Owens, William A. "Bill," 119, 119n189

Patuxent River Naval Air Station, 17, 17n37, 107
Peleliu, Battle of, 18n42
Pensacola Naval Air Station, 19, 19n45
Perry, William J., 95, 95n151
Philippines, 26
physical fitness: influence of Marines on carriers, 71, 77–78; interest in and improvement of, 72–74; Marines fitness levels, 71, 77–78; running habits and running marathons, 73–74, 95–96; smoking ban and policy, 71–73; standards for, 73
Pirie, Robert B., Jr. "Robin," 58, 58n101, 115, 115n186
Pirie, Robert Burns, 58–59, 58n102
pizza place at Rolling Valley Mall, 28–29, 29n65, 31
Powell, Colin Luther, 97, 97n154, 127

purple to designate joint commands and billets, 89, 89n147

Quantico Marine Corps Base, 64, 64n110

Ralston, Joseph W. "Joe," 99, 99n159
readiness and interdeployment training cycle, 115–18
respectful relationships and earning respect, 44, 110
Rogers, Roy (Leonard Franklin Slye), 4, 4n14
Rolling Valley Mall pizza place, 28–29, 29n65, 31
Roosevelt, Theodore, 4n12
running habits and running marathons, 73–74, 95–96
Ryan, John R., 16, 16n36
Ryan, Michael E., 108n177

"Saigon Execution" (Adams), 29n64, 31
Schmitt, John, 79
"From the Sea" white paper, 114–15, 114n183, 114–15n185
Second Fleet: command of, 79–87; interdeployment training cycle, 115–18; operational area for, 79n126
senior-level school, 60
Shelton, Henry Hugh, 80, 80n131, 83
Sidra, Gulf of, 46–48, 46n83, 47nn84–86
Silver Star, 13n30, 38n78, 74n119
Sixth Fleet: El Dorado Canyon operation, 50; operational area for, 50n89; operations officer for, 55, 56, 58
Slye, Leonard Franklin (Roy Rogers), 4, 4n14
smoking ban and policy, 71–73
Sons of the Pioneers, 4, 4n14
South Dakota, 4, 4nn11–12
South Vietnamese expatriates, success of, 28–31
Soviet Union: communication with Soviet pilots, 36; escort of Soviet bombers, 35–37
Special Operations Aviation Regiment, 160th, 80, 80nn133–134, 86
Special Ops fastboat trip to *Mount Whitney*, 86–87
Spencer, Tim, 4n14
Stearman biplane, 22
"Steer by the Stars" vision statement, 96, 96n153, 99, 103, 111
Stevens, Theodore Fulton, Sr. "Ted," 102, 102n163
Strategic Studies Group (SSG), Naval War College,, 57–60, 57nn99–100, 58n101, 59n103, 114–15, 114n184, 115n186
Striking Fleet Atlantic (SFL), 79–87, 79n127

T-2 Buckeye aircraft, 19, 19n47
T-33 Shooting Star trainer aircraft, 2n2
Tactical Fighter Wing, 20th, 52n94
Tactical Fighter Wing, 48th, 52n94
Tailhook Association Symposium: career terminations and price paid by naval aviation, 66–69;

orders to go to for panel presentation, 65–66; press reporting about scandal, 66, 68; professional aspect of, 66; recovery from scandal, 69; scandal related to, 64–69, 64n109

Theodore Roosevelt, 70–73, 70n112, 75–79, 75n120

Third Fleet: interdeployment training cycle, 115–18; operational area for, 115n187

Thunderbirds, 5, 5n16

Title X, U.S. Code, 103, 103n166, 118

transitions, attitude toward, 126–29

Tripoli, 49–54

Trost, Carlisle Albert Herman "Carl," 59–60, 59n105

Tupolev Tu-16 Badger bombers, 36, 36n76

Tupolev Tu-95 Bear bombers, 35–37, 35n75

University of Wisconsin, 9

Uphold Democracy, Operation, 79nn128–129, 80n131

Urgent Fury, Operation, 85, 85nn143–145

V-22 Osprey aircraft, 107–8, 107n173, 109

Venlet, David "DJ," 47, 47n86

VF-84 Jolly Rogers squadron, 42–44, 42n80, 46, 58

VF-101 Grim Reapers squadron, 38–39, 38n77

VF-142 Ghostriders squadron, 34–37, 34n73

VF-191 Hellcats squadron, 22–27

Vietnam War: anti-military attitudes during, 39–40; attitude about while at Naval Academy, 8–9, 8n20; classmates recognized for heroism during, 13nn29–30; Denton as POW during, 60n107; Dixie Station, 24, 24n58; Easter Offensive, 24, 24n59; first-class cruise during, 17–18, 17n41, 18nn42–44; morale in Navy at the end of, 39; *Oriskany* combat cruises during, 22–28, 25n60; Yankee Station, 17, 17n41, 24

virtual presence, 124–25

Vought F-8/F-8J Crusader aircraft, 20n51, 23–24, 23n56, 33, 34

Walberg, Peter Elon, 7, 7n18

warfare: SSG work on future warfare applications, 59–60; strategic-level thinking for future concepts, 63

Washington, George, 4n12

Webb, James H., Jr. "Jim," 13, 13n29

West Point (Military Academy, U.S.), 3, 3n6

West Salem, Wisconsin, 2, 2n1, 4, 7, 7n18

When Hell Was In Session (Denton), 60n107

women: integration into force at sea, 110; Naval Academy admission of, 14

World War II: destroyer escort activities during, 10n22, 11; 8th Air Force role in, 2n5; father's military service during, 2–3, 2nn2–5

www.ingramcontent.com/pod-product-compliance
Lightning Source LLC
Chambersburg PA
CBHW080612170426
43209CB00007B/1407